Music in the Andes

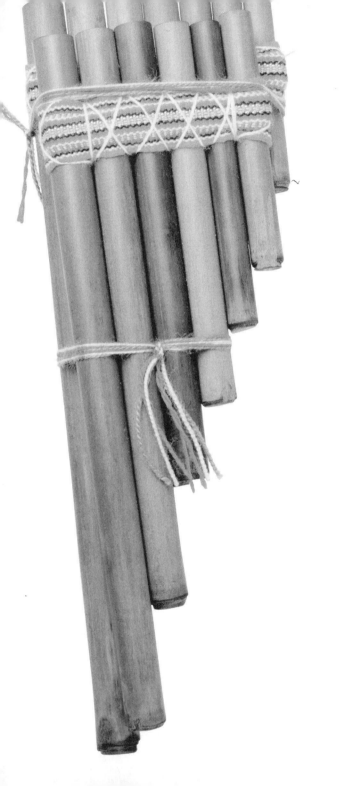

Music in the Andes

∽

EXPERIENCING MUSIC, EXPRESSING CULTURE

∽

THOMAS TURINO

New York   Oxford
OXFORD UNIVERSITY PRESS
2008

Oxford University Press, Inc., publishes works that further Oxford University's objective of excellence in research, scholarship, and education.

Oxford   New York
Auckland   Cape Town   Dar es Salaam   Hong Kong   Karachi
Kuala Lumpur   Madrid   Melbourne   Mexico City   Nairobi
New Delhi   Shanghai   Taipei   Toronto

With offices in
Argentina   Austria   Brazil   Chile   Czech Republic   France   Greece
Guatemala   Hungary   Italy   Japan Poland   Portugal   Singapore
South Korea   Switzerland   Thailand   Turkey   Ukraine   Vietnam

Published by Oxford University press, Inc.
198 Madison Avenue, New York, New York 10016
http://www.oup.com

Library of Congress Cataloging-in-Publication Data
Turino, Thomas.
   Music in the Andes : experiencing music, expressing culture / Thomas Turino.
      p. cm. — (Global music series)
   Includes bibliographical references and index.
   ISBN 978-0-19-530674-3 (paper (main)) — ISBN 978-0-19-530673-6 (cloth)
   1. Music—Andes Region—History and criticism. I. Title.

ML3575.A475T87 2008
780.98—dc22   200723300

Printing number: 9 8 7 6 5 4 3 2 1

Printed in the United States of America
on acid-free paper

GLOBAL MUSIC SERIES

General Editors: Bonnie C. Wade and Patricia Shehan Campbell

Music in East Africa, Gregory Barz
Music in Central Java, Benjamin Brinner
Teaching Music Globally, Patricia Shehan Campbell
Native American Music in Eastern North America, Beverley Diamond
Carnival Music in Trinidad, Shannon Dudley
Music in Bali, Lisa Gold
Music in Ireland, Dorothea E. Hast and Stanley Scott
Music in China, Frederick Lau
Music in Egypt, Scott L. Marcus
Music in Brazil, John P. Murphy
Music in America, Adelaida Reyes
Music in Bulgaria, Timothy Rice
Music in North India, George E. Ruckert
Mariachi Music in America, Daniel Sheehy
Music in West Africa, Ruth M. Stone
Music in the Andes, Thomas Turino
Music in South India, T. Viswanathan and Matthew Harp Allen
Music in Japan, Bonnie C. Wade
Thinking Musically, Bonnie C. Wade

*For my parents Betty and Joe, who set me in motion
and guided me along the way*

Contents

Foreword   ix
Preface   xi
CD Track List   xvii

1. **Indigenous Wind Ensembles and Community**   1
   Indigenous Identity and Aymara Social Style   4
   Musical Style   8
   Participatory Music Making in Conima   20
   Festivals in Conima   26
   Año Nuevo   27
   San Isidro (May 14–15)   33

2. *Charango* **String Traditions**   38
   The Indigenous *Charango* of Canas, Cusco   39
   The *Mestizo Charango*   54
   Indigenous and *Mestizo* Styles Compared   68

3. **Dance Dramas in** *Mestizo* **Catholic Festivals**   71
   The Virgin of Carmen   81
   Festival Activities   82
   The Dance Troupes   87

4. **Andean Music in Andean Cities: The Case of Lima, Peru**   97
   Nationalism in the 1920s   99
   Regional "Country Music" in Lima   103
   Highland Regional Associations   110

Chicha Music and the Children of
    Andean Migrants 118
Technocumbia 121

5. **Andean Music in the Cities of the World** 124
    Cosmopolitanism as a Type of
        Cultural Formation 127
    From Buenos Aires and Paris to the
        Cities of the World 130
    "Andean Folkloric Music" in the Andes 134

Glossary *139*
References *145*
Resources *148*
Index *151*

Foreword

In the past three decades interest in music around the world has surged, as evidenced in the proliferation of courses at the college level, the burgeoning "world music" market in the recording business, and the extent to which musical performance is evoked as a lure in the international tourist industry. This heightened interest has encouraged an explosion in ethnomusicological research and publication, including production of reference works and textbooks. The original model for the "world music" course—if this is Tuesday, this must be Japan—has grown old, as has the format of textbooks for it, either a series of articles in single multiauthored volumes that subscribe to the idea of "a survey" and have created a canon of cultures for study, or single-authored studies purporting to cover world musics or ethnomusicology. The time has come for a change.

This Global Music Series offers a new paradigm. Instructors can now design their own courses; choosing from a set of case study volumes, they can decide which and how much music they will teach. The series also does something else; rather than uniformly taking a large region and giving superficial examples from several different countries within it, case studies offer two formats—some focused on a specific culture, some on a discrete geographical area. In either case, each volume offers greater depth than the usual survey. Themes significant in each instance guide the choice of music that is discussed. The contemporary musical situation is the point of departure in all the volumes, with historical information and traditions covered as they elucidate the present. In addition, a set of unifying topics such as gender, globalization, and authenticity occur throughout the series. These are addressed in the framing volume, *Thinking Musically* (Wade), which sets the stage for the case studies by introducing those topics and other ways to think about how people make music meaningful and useful in their lives. *Thinking Musically* also presents the basic elements of music as they are practiced in musical systems around the world so that authors of each case study do not have to spend time explaining them and can delve immediately into the particular music. A second framing volume, *Teaching Music*

Globally (Campbell), guides teachers in the use of *Thinking Musically* and the case studies.

The series subtitle, "Experiencing Music, Expressing Culture," also puts in the forefront the people who make music or in some other way experience it and also through it express shared culture. This resonance with global studies in such disciplines as history and anthropology, with their focus on processes and themes that permit cross-study, occasions the title of this Global Music Series.

Bonnie C. Wade
Patricia Shehan Campbell
General Editors

Preface

During the month of June 2004, hundreds of dance and music groups came from their rural communities and urban neighborhoods to perform in the central plaza of Cusco city, once the capital of the Inca Empire and still the jewel of Peru. Some community musicians played indigenous flutes used in the region since long before the arrival of Europeans in the 1530s. Others played stringed instruments such as the diatonic harp, violin, and mandolin introduced to the Andes during the colonial period, in combination with later arrivals such as the accordion. Brass bands, popularized during the nineteenth century, also accompanied costumed dances that have their roots in medieval Europe and pre-Hispanic Peru but which are created anew to comment on local histories as recent as the late twentieth-century tourist boom.

During the same month, there was a three-day rock festival in Cusco with bands from different parts of Peru and Latin America drawing thousands of young middle-class music fans from the city and beyond. The bands played in a variety of styles ranging from what North Americans might call soft and hard rock to jazz fusion to new local combinations of Andean flutes and electrified *charangos* (a small local guitar variant) with electric guitars, bass, and drum sets. The rock festival, sponsored by a local beer company, took place in the new fairgrounds with a well-equipped stage, a huge sound system, lights, and kiosks selling food and beer. The kids in tee shirts and jeans stood packed together in front of the stage—some dancing, some too rowdy for the crowded space. At first glance, these fans and the sounds that pounded out from the stage could have been anywhere in the world where capitalist cosmopolitanism has become influential.

In addition to all this, Cusco has had composers working in the European classical tradition who produced pieces in step with elite European trends ranging from baroque music during the colonial period to the twentieth-century avant-garde. In 2004, Cusco had a nightclub totally dedicated to jazz. In June 2004, local neighborhood and town parties sometimes centered around bands with electric keyboards and drum machines that played a local Peruvian variant of *cumbia* music, a genre that began in Colombia but by now has been popularized throughout the Americas. During the same month, old women could be heard singing religious hymns in Quechua, the major indigenous language of the region, as well as in Spanish for particular Catholic saints in churches in the city and nearby towns. In the streets, plazas, and restaurants where tourists gather, other groups could be heard playing panpipes, *kenas* (indigenous Andean flutes), *charangos*, guitars, and Argentinean *bombos* (drums) in the "folkloric Andean style" that has become well known throughout the cosmopolitan world—a style that originated in the 1950s among musicians traveling between Buenos Aires, Argentina, and Paris, France. Having already heard this music in subways, at festivals, and on records at home, this is the style that most foreign visitors associate with the region; and local musicians are all too happy to learn to play it for the tourist dollars that it can earn.

The Andes remains one of the richest and most diverse musical areas of Latin America. Unlike places where newer musical styles replace older traditions that then fade from memory, in southern Peru it seems that each new musical layer gets added, recombined, and performed alongside earlier musical traditions—new innovations only adding to the richness of the whole. In addition to this historically produced diversity, there is major regional diversity, with neighboring areas sometimes having an almost completely different inventory of instruments, songs, and dances. As demonstrated throughout the book, and especially in Chapter 4, Peruvians strongly identify with their regions of origin and the distinctiveness of regional musical styles serves to express and sustain regional identities.

Finally, distinct musical values, practices, and styles articulate with the sensibilities of different social groups in the Andean highlands. People living in or hailing from indigenous communities might still distinguish themselves through dress, music, and broader patterns of living from *mestizos*, individuals whose cultural habits derive from indigenous, European, and cosmopolitan models. Terms such as *criollo* (Euro-American), *vecino* (literally "neighbor" but meaning town dweller), and *gente decent* (decent people) are sometimes used to refer to people of high social standing in any particular environment. These and other social categories are largely based on cultural lifeways as well as class. Since people can change their cultural habits and can move up economically, they are relative, fluid categories but still may be used for convenience to indicate general tendencies for living.

This book introduces contemporary indigenous, *mestizo*, and urban musical traditions of the Andes from the perspective of a series of selected Peruvian case studies in Chapters 1–4. The final chapter describes the emergence of "Andean folkloric music," a cosmopolitan tradition that has become influential throughout the Andean countries and by now is performed in subways, streets, and festivals in different parts of the world. As a primary theme uniting the different chapters, the presentation underscores the dynamic interplay of historical continuities, musical innovation, and the sociopolitical relations that brought new musical innovations and social identities into play. As another prominent theme, the traditions presented illustrate the special *communicative* potentials of music, dance, and festival to articulate "ethnic," class, regional, "national," and gendered identities as well as the distinctive cultural sensibilities and histories that underpin identity. The use of music and dance to maintain specific communities, the influence of regional and class identifications on musical styles, and the special problems of creating a national identification in Peru are prominent themes that resurface throughout the book.

As in most places, music is also used to communicate across seemingly uncrossable divides such as those between humans and the supernatural and between courting adolescents in love. As a prime articulation of identity and worldview, the Andean music cases discussed show the complex interplay among social groups at the local community, regional, state, and trans-state levels and between rural and urban environments. While the same instruments and pieces that once articulated rural community identities may now be heard in New York, Tokyo, and Paris, music is *not* a universal language nor has Andean music become "global." The cases presented here illustrate that the sound and meaning of the music change radically as it moves into new social spheres and that the folkloric form of Andean music, the main one to reach cosmopolitan audiences, was cosmopolitan at its inception.

As a final theme, this book explores the ethical and stylistic differences between music making in communal participatory occasions and staged presentational performance as yet another type of diversity that helps distinguish and define various types of Andean music. There are many ways to participate with music, including listening silently to a concert or daydreaming to tunes on an iPod while walking back from class. In this book, however, I use the concept of "participatory music" in the restricted sense of actively taking part in music making and dance. Moreover, *participatory music* is defined by contexts where everyone is invited, and often expected, to participate musically or by dancing and where there are no clear-cut artist–audience distinctions, only participants and potential participants. Musical styles and practices are shaped in special ways when a primary goal is to involve as many people in performing as possible. In contrast, *presentational music* is defined here as an ideal type where one group of actors, the musicians or performers, prepare and present music/dance to another group, the audience, who are not primarily involved in producing the sound and motion of the performance. The responsibilities and goals of presentational performance inspire practices and style features that contrast with participatory performance, as will be illustrated throughout this book.

Conceptualizing participatory and presentational music making as distinct fields of practice invites us to think about music as more than mere sounds and styles; these concepts require us to attend to the values, goals, and modes of social interaction that guide musical experience and the very notion of what music is and is for. In the Andean context, participatory music correlates most prominently with indigenous lifeways and ethics that stand as a modern alternative to capitalist cosmopolitanism, a cultural formation in which presentational and recorded musics are most highly valued. But by now, indigenous musicians also record and perform in presentational contexts such as state-sponsored folklore festivals; conversely, *mestizo* musicians perform in both participatory events, such as family parties, as well as presentational stage events. It will also become apparent that certain traditions, such as the Aymara *satiri* dance (Chapter 1), fall somewhere in between the ideal types and that the Paucartambo festival (Chapter 3) frequently shifts between the presentational and participatory modes. Thus, these two fields are intended as general conceptual guides for analyzing specific instances of performance rather than as hard-and-fast rubrics for categorizing musical traditions. Nonetheless, the participatory–presentational contrast provides important tools for thinking about major cultural tendencies that distinguish the diverse social groups involved with Andean music.

I lived in southern Peru for approximately four years between 1977 and 1986, studying with musicians and doing research on a variety of musical traditions. I have taken two shorter trips to the region since then, most recently in 2004. Many of the stories in this book are derived from that work and so must be placed in historical and regional perspective. It is my hope that this brief introduction to Andean music will inspire new ways of thinking about what music is and can do for people and might even inspire some to travel to the region to experience the place, its wonderful people, and its remarkable music for themselves.

ACKNOWLEDGMENTS

I would like to thank Bonnie Wade and Pat Cambell for the invitation to contribute to this series. I would also like to thank the Benavente and Apaza families for their continuing friendship, and all my Peruvian teachers and friends including Ernesto Valdez and David Fuentes, F. Calderon, and Raul Borquez. Julia Chambi kindly shared her father's photographs with me and gave permission to use them for educational purposes. Finally, special thanks go to my wife Amy, who helped in more ways—technical and spiritual—than I can name. Thanks to the Research Board of the University of Illinois for material support for this project.

CD Track List

1. *Tarkas* of Huata Community, Carnival in Conima, 1986.
2. Qhantati Ururi of Ayllu Sulcata, *siku lento* genre, "Edith," composed by Filiberto Calderon, 22 players.
3. Qhantati Ururi of Ayllu Sulcata, *siku ligero*, "Egenio" composed by Filiberto Calderon, 22 players.
4. Qhantati Ururi of Ayllu Sulcata, *siku choclo* genre, circa 50 players, Easter 1985.
5. Ayllu Sulcata, *siku imillani* genre, May 1985.
6. Ayllu Cambria, *pitu* ensemble, *Achachk'umu* dance, May 3, 1986.
7. Ayllu Japisi, five-hole *pinkillus*, *Candelaria* Festival, 1986.
8. Ayllu Sulcata, *siku satiri* genre, *San Isidro*, May 15, 1986.
9. Manuel Quispe, Caneño *pinkullu* solo.
10. Paulina Wilka, "Punchay Kashua" song.
11. Paulina Wilka and Manuel Quispe, vocal/*pinkullu* duet.
12. Raul Quispe, *charango*/vocal, "Tuta Kashua" in the plaza Descanso, Canas, 1982.
13. Severino Piñeda, *charango*/vocal, "Papa Tarpuy." Canas, 1982.
14. Julio Benavente, *charango*, Raul Bohorquez, guitar, "Sonquito Corazoncito," *wayno*.
15. J. Benavente and R. Bohorquez, "La Mala Yerba," *wayno* by J. Benavente.
16. J. Benavente "Descansa Corazon Fatigado" *yaraví*, with *fuga de wayno* "Cuando te conocí."
17. Ernesto Valdez, *charango*, David Fuentes, guitar, "Marinera Cusqueña."
18. E. Valdez, *charango*, D. Fuentes, guitar, "Yo te perdono," *vals criollo*.

19. *Chuncho* music, two transverse flutes, snare and bass drums.

20. *Qolla* song to the *Virgin del Carmen*, accompanied by *orquesta cusqueña* (*kenas*, violin, harp, accordion, mandolin, drum).

21. *Majeños* dance music, brass band.

22. *Majeños'* brass band playing the *yaraví*, "Gentil Gaviota" for the Virgin during the opening of the festival.

23. *Qhapac Negros*, song for the Virgin, accompanied by *orquesta* (*kenas*, violin, accordion, harp, mandolin and drum).

24. *Qollas* song "Chas Kas Chay," with *orquesta*.

25. Pastorita Huaracina, "Quisiera Olvidarte," *wayno*. Courtesy Iempsa.

26. Picaflor de los Andes, "Gorrioncito," *wayno* by Victor A. Gil. Courtesy Arhoolie Records, www.arhoolie.com. All Rights Reserved.

27. Trio Lira Paucina, "Vengo del Prado," *wayno*. Courtesy Iempsa.

28. Centro Social Conima (regional club in Lima), "Rosaura," *siku lento*, 20 players.

29. Los Destellos, "Valicha," *wayno* from Cusco played as *chicha*.

30. Julio Benavente, *charango*, "Valicha," *wayno* from Cusco.

31. Los Shapis, "Somos Estudiantes," *chicha*.

32. Joven Sensación, "Tic, Tic, Tac," *technocumbia*. A full version of this song is available for purchase at iTunes.

33. Urubamba, "Kachapari," cosmopolitan "folkloric music," *wayno*. (P) Notice and "Under license from The SONY BMG Custom Marketing Group, SONY BMG MUSIC ENTERTAINMENT."

34. Urubamba, "Campanas de Santa Cruz," Andean "folkloric music." (P) Notice and "Under license from The SONY BMG Custom Marketing Group, SONY BMG MUSIC ENTERTAINMENT."

CHAPTER 1

Indigenous Wind Ensembles and Community

Early rainy-season morning, mist rolls off Lake Titicaca; it is damp and just cold enough to see your breath. A handful of middle-aged men stand huddled on the knoll, which is their usual meeting place. It is too early. These groggy musicians are the same ones who stayed up all the night before composing *tarka* pieces for this year's carnival festival. Jorge impatiently beats the bass drum loudly every five minutes or so, calling the community together. Men and women gradually straggle onto the knoll over the next hour and a half dressed in their best clothes— some hats decorated with flowers, some dresses, jackets, and ponchos decorated with paper streamers. When about twelve men show up with *tarkas*, a square wooden flute with a whistle (or duct) mouthpiece, they begin to play through some tunes composed in past years and to run through the new pieces composed the night before (Figure 1.1, CD track 1). More community members gather. As the volume picks up, people in their nearby homes realize that the group is about to set off for the district capital town of Conima to make their entrance. The *ayllu* (indigenous community) headman of Putina and his wife arrive to lead the procession to the town plaza, and about thirty people start the mile walk led by the *tarka* musicians who play all the way (Figure 1.2).

At the entrance to the plaza, the people of Putina wait once again for more late-comers to arrive so that they can make their most forceful entrance. On other streets leading into the plaza different *ayllu* groups are doing the same. For Carnival, it is customary for indigenous communities to perform in the town plaza for the opening two days and the closing day of the week-long festival and to perform for themselves in their own communities in the intervening days. As more people assemble, the Aymara musicians from Putina run through the new composition that they had selected for the entrance so that musicians who had not attended last night's rehearsal could learn it quickly for

1

FIGURE 1.1   Tarka *ensemble from the community of Putina meeting on the morning before the opening of Carnival.*

the entrance. Once in the plaza, the different communities take part in a kind of informal competition to see who has the most dancers, who has the most innovative new compositions, and who can play loudest and longest.

In Conima during the mid-1980s, festival performances occurred on the average of once a month somewhere in the district and were the joyous, boisterous counterpoint to the hard and somewhat solitary tasks of daily peasant life. Since participation in festival performance

FIGURE 1.2 *Tarkas de Putina walking to town to perform in the plaza for Carnival.*

is totally voluntary, the size, volume, and strength of a particular *ayllu*'s performing group are direct indices of community solidarity and spirit; in bad economic years or when there are problems in a community, fewer people show up. When an *ayllu* splits due to social problems, one of the first public signs of the two new social groups is that each will send its own separate performing ensemble to the plaza for major festivals. The makeup of particular ensembles—who plays and dances with whom—thus clearly communicates the membership of given communities. In the District of Conima, festival music making and dancing are the main way that Aymara communities strengthen and celebrate their internal unity and represent community identity to others.

This chapter describes indigenous music, dance, and festival among Aymara speakers in the District of Conima, Puno, Peru, as an example of one of the many types of localized indigenous musical traditions in the Andean region. The wind ensembles described for Conima more closely resemble the types of music making and ensembles found in Bolivia than they do the styles found farther north in Peru and Ecuador.

As a major theme of this chapter, I will investigate the ways broader patterns of local social style and ethics articulate with participatory musical performance and the ways music and dance function to communicate—with spiritual forces, among different communities, and among the members of the same community.

INDIGENOUS IDENTITY AND AYMARA SOCIAL STYLE

The term *Aymara* refers to the second most commonly spoken indigenous language in the Andes, after Quechua. In Ecuador, much of Peru, and parts of Bolivia, highland indigenous people speak Quechua. Aymara is spoken in the most southern parts of Peru and in Bolivia. The terms *Quechua* and *Aymara* do not denote sociopolitical groups, 'nations,' or 'tribes' akin to Navajo and Hopi in North America. Up until recently, and in many places still, indigenous Andeans identify most strongly with their *ayllu* and their local region. In recent decades, however, social movements for First Nations or Native American rights in the central Andean countries of Ecuador, Peru, and Bolivia have begun to inspire broader indigenous-group identifications in relation to negotiating with and seeking aid from governments and nongovernmental aid organizations. In such contexts *Quechua, Aymara,* and other terms denoting languages are sometimes used as *'ethnic'* (subnational cultural) group designations. Moreover, at different times since the 1920s, the governments of Andean countries have made efforts through economic reforms and cultural and educational programs to get indigenous people to identify with their 'nation-states' (i.e., to think of themselves as part of the 'nation'), with varying degrees of success.

It is generally understood that social identities are always multiple and situationally relative. The same person can identify with her family, community, school, region, others of the same gender or social class, as well as an 'ethnic' designation or country depending on the

ACTIVITY 1.1 *Take ten minutes and make a list of all the different aspects of yourself that you think are important for defining who you are (e.g., age, gender, occupation, religion, sports, hobbies, family, nationality, clothing and musical styles, etc.). Place these in*

one column. Do all these aspects of your identity come into play in every social situation? Jot down, in an adjoining column, one or two social situations where each aspect of identity that you listed might come to the fore as most important either to you or the people you are interacting with.

goals and salient nodes of identity within a particular situation. People also have cultural habits in common with others along these different lines of identification to varying degrees as the result of common life experiences. These general principles of identity formation are true for people in Conima as well.

In Conima, indigenous people most strongly identify with their *ayllu* and with their region, defined by the District of Conima primarily as well as the Province of Huancané, in which the district is located, and the Department of Puno, of which the province is a part (Figure 1.3). If a major soccer match is coming up, however, Conimeños might also identity with the 'national' Peruvian team. In the Andes, regional identities strongly articulate with distinctive regional lifeways, especially clothing and music/dance styles, as well as patterns of social organization and interaction. Huancané is one of two Aymara-speaking provinces in the Department of Puno. Men from Huancané can be identified by a black and red–striped poncho, and the same instruments and dances are common throughout the province, distinguishing Huancaneños from people in neighboring regions.

The District of Conima is located on the shores of the great highland lake Titicaca and on the Bolivian border in a region called the *altiplano*, or high plain. The majority of the population in the district speaks Aymara and lives in the rural *ayllus* as peasant agriculturalists and herders. Indigenous families often have members who have moved to cities elsewhere in Peru and in other countries and so are in contact with these other places through their kin. The district capital town of Conima is inhabited by people who consider themselves to be of a higher social class than *ayllu* dwellers (Figure 1.4). They typically refer to themselves as *vecinos* or variably as *mestizos*; the most elite among them might refer to themselves as *criollo*. The *vecinos* work as teachers, merchants, and administrators. During my stay, social hierarchy and tension between the *vecinos* and *ayllu* dwellers was pronounced. In fiestas, only *vecinos*

FIGURE 1.3   *Map of Peru.*

were invited inside the private parties sometimes held in *vecino* homes, and indigenous friends of mine often avoided social interactions with *vecinos* when possible. This pattern of social prejudice, segregation, and subjugation of indigenous people has a long history and can be generalized for other parts of the Andes.

Indigenous communities in Conima have an ethical value system and social style that has been described more broadly for Aymara

FIGURE 1.4   *The town of Conima.*

communities in Bolivia by the anthropologist Javier Albó (1974). Within indigenous Aymara communities, most social relationships are organized around egalitarian principles. This does not mean that everyone is equal in all ways. Certain families have more land or animals or are better farmers; certain people have special knowledge about rituals, healing, music, or making things; elders are granted particular respect; in the public political sphere, men seem to have more say, with women often expressing their views indirectly through their husbands; men play musical instruments and women do not. By "egalitarian" I mean that there are no formal structures or institutions of coercion or control through which certain individuals can force their will on others. Because of the models for social interaction that they grow up with, most Conimeños do not *want* to assert their own will against the will of others. This simple fact has a variety of social and musical ramifications.

The political leadership of specific *ayllus* rotates frequently among married couples, and successful leadership involves a style of gentle guiding rather than firm command. Decision making requires group consensus; since no one has the power to force anyone to do something against their will, everyone has to agree with a particular decision or project if full participation is needed. In keeping with egalitarian principles, individuals do not like to stand out in group settings and the group is emphasized over the individual. For the most part, people within communities avoid conflict whenever possible. Since music making is a collective social activity, it should come as no surprise that all these habits of Conimeño social style guide musical practices and style as well.

MUSICAL STYLE

By the mid-1980s, indigenous community ensembles mainly played five types of indigenous wind instruments with drum accompaniment. Each wind instrument is played in ensemble only with the same type, and each is associated with different festivals and times of year.

Sikus are a type of instrument played in the region since before the arrival of the Spanish in the 1530s. *Sikus* are double-row panpipes, on which the pitch series alternates between the two rows (each row contains a series of thirds). Each row is played by a musician who *interlocks*, or *hockets*, his pitches with his partner to complete a melody; i.e., a single instrument requires two players. The panpipe row with six tubes is called *ira* (the one that leads), and the row with seven tubes is called *arca* (the one that follows). In a highly stylized and foregrounded way, the musical practice of interlocking both requires and articulates the close cooperation and reciprocity that underpins Conimeño social life more generally.

ACTIVITY 1.2 *If the song "Row, Row, Row Your Boat" was played on* sikus, *the melody would be divided between the* ira *and* arca *rows in the following way. With a couple of friends or room-mates, divide into group 1 (*ira *part) and group 2 (*arca *part) and then sing: 1—Row, row, row; 2—your; 1—boat, gent; 2—ly; 1—down; 2—the; 1—stream; 2—merrily; 1—merrily, merrily, merrily, life; 2—is; 1—but; 2—a; 1—dream. Begin by practicing slowly to render the parts correctly and then increasingly speed up to get a sense of how a tightly interlocked performance feels.*

In Conima, *siku* ensembles include up to nine different sizes of pan-pipes cut to play in parallel octaves, fifths, and thirds; and ensembles typically range from around twenty-four to fifty players (see Wade 2004:88–103 for a discussion of melodic and harmonic intervals). Between four and six *siku* players also accompany the group with large double-headed drums known as *bombos* or *wankaras* (Figure 1.5). The harmonic voicing differs for panpipe ensembles in different regions of Puno and Bolivia, and these styles are recognized as signs of regional identity (e.g., the District of Conima versus other neighboring districts) and, thus, function in a parallel way to regional clothing styles. Throughout the southern Andes, many indigenous instruments are associated with either the dry season (April–October) or the rainy season (November–March). *Sikus* are associated with dry-season festivals beginning with Easter and concluding with the Fiesta of San Miguel

FIGURE 1.5 Siku *ensemble Qhantati Ururi of* ayllu *Sulcata, walking into the plaza of Conima. Notice the large* bombos *(drums) and the different-sized panpipes; e.g., in the back of the group two men play long panpipes and the men directly in front of them play shorter instruments. Guías Filiberto Calderón and Aldamir Calderón play* bombos *and middle-sized panpipes (front right).*

(September 28–30). *Sikus* are also played at weddings, which can occur throughout the year.

Sikus are used to play a variety of genres, but the two most common types of pieces are identified by tempi and are simply called *waynos lentos* and *waynos ligeros*, or slow pieces and fast pieces (CD tracks 2 and 3). These genres have the same seven-tone scale that begins with a minor third (see Wade, 2004:88–90). Unlike in North America, where this type of minor sound is associated with sad, somber, or serious emotions, it has no such emotional meanings for indigenous Andean people. Rather, slow tempi communicate more serious or profound sentiments and fast pieces are associated with upbeat emotions. In addition to tempo, these two genres are distinguished by different cadence formulas that conclude major sections. Most sections of fast pieces conclude with a quick alternation between the *ira* and *arca* players, a formula known as *chuta chuta*. *Lentos* have a drawn-out chord for the cadences. Like the vast majority of music in Conima, *lentos* and *ligeros* are comprised of three relatively short repeated sections, or AABBCC form. In these genres, the cadence formulas occur between all sections except between the second B section and the first C section and between the C sections.

ACTIVITY 1.3 *Listen to CD tracks 2 and 3 following the seconds counter on your CD player to study the form of these pieces by identifying the different sections and the concluding or cadence formulas charted for the first repetition of each piece. Learn to sing the melody of each, and after listening to the first repetition several times with the timeline provided, complete the chart for subsequent repetitions of the piece.*

CD track 2, wayno lento

00:00	Introductory "chord"
00:03	A section, cadence formula at 00:14
00:16	A section, cadence formula at 00:27
00:29	B section, cadence formula at 00:36
00:38	B section
00:46	C section
00:52	C section, cadence formula at 00:57
00:59	A section (begins the second repetition of the piece)

CD track 3, wayno ligero

00:04   *Chuta chuta* formula, introduction
00:06   A section, *chuta chuta* cadence at 00:17
00:18   A section, *chuta chuta* cadence at 00:29
00:31   B section, *chuta chuta* cadence at 00:41
00:43   B section
00:54   C section
01:03   C section, *chuta chuta* cadence at 01:11
01:12   A section (begins the second repetition of the piece)

For the Easter celebration, *waynos ligeros* are performed with bass and snare drums rather than *bombos* and with this minor alteration in instrumentation are considered a different genre, called *choclo* (CD track 4); notice that the *chuta chuta* cadence formula remains the same as in the *ligero* (CD track 3). *Imillani* is another genre performed by *siku* ensembles for the "coming out" of young girls of marriageable age. These pieces are distinguished from the *lentos* and *ligeros* (and *choclos*) by the use of a major sounding scale and a different cadence formula which occurs between all sections (CD track 5).

ACTIVITY 1.4   *Study the time chart for the first repetition of* imillani *(CD track 5), learn to sing the melody, and then complete the chart. Notice that the form is slightly different from* lentos *and* ligeros *in that the quick cadence formula follows every section and the sections are shorter. Notice the different quality of the melody because of the use of a different (major) scale compared to track 2 by singing both melodies one after the other.*

CD track 5, imillani

00:01   Introductory formula
00:03   A section, cadence formula at 00:06
00:07   A section, cadence formula at 00:11
00:12   B section, cadence formula at 00:16

00:17   B section, cadence formula at 00:20
00:21   C section, cadence formula at 00:25
00:26   C section, cadence formula at 00:29
01:30   A section (begins the second repetition of the piece)

Transverse six-hole cane flutes known as *pitus* are played in *consorts* (groups of instruments tuned together) of three sizes in parallel fourths, fifths, and octaves accompanied by snare and base drums (Figure 1.6). Side-blown cane flutes are found throughout the Andes, although often played in smaller groups than the twelve or more musicians who play in ensemble in Conima. *Pitus* are largely associated with costumed dance dramas, especially during Christmas and Santa Cruz (May 3) and for wedding processions; thus, this instrument does not have a seasonal association. There is some evidence that transverse

FIGURE 1.6   Pitu *ensemble from* ayllu *Checasaya, Conima.*

flutes were played on the north coast of Peru in the pre-Columbian period, but European transverse flutes are just as likely a source for their current widespread diffusion. Throughout the Andes, they are typically overblown to produce the high pitch ranges that Andeans favor generally (CD track 6). Another common feature of music in Conima, and of indigenous Andean music more widely, is the intensive repetition of *motives* (short repeated melodic units) across different sections. This can be heard in the *pitu* piece on CD track 6, where the same motive (x) leads into the cadence of each section; notice that a C section is little more than a repetition of this same motive. This particular rhythmic–melodic motive correlates with a backward hopping step in the *Achachk'umu* dance.

CD track 6, pitu *ensemble*, Achachk'umu *dance*

00:02	Held note that serves as intro
00:03	A section, cadence motive (x) at 00:10
00:13	A section, cadence motive (x) at 00:20
00:22	B section, cadence motive (x) at 00:29
00:32	B section, cadence motive (x) at 00:39
00:40	C section, cadence motive (x) at 00:42
00:43	C section, cadence motive (x) at 00:45
00:47	Held note that begins the form
00:48	A section (begins the second repetition)

Duct flutes (with mouthpieces like a whistle or recorder), the other main instrument type in Conima, are associated with rainy-season festivals from *Todos los Santos* (All-Saints' Day) through the Carnival season. There are three duct flutes used in Conima: five- and six-hole *pinkillus* and *tarkas* (Figure 1.7). *Pinkullo* is a pre-Hispanic Quechua term referring to vertical flutes generally, and it is still used in various Andean regions in this way. *Pinkillu* is the Aymara term that refers specifically to cane vertical duct flutes. Both the five- and six-hole *pinkillus* are played in a "wide unison" (some players blowing slightly higher and slightly lower than the median pitch series) in large ensembles of up to thirty musicians accompanied by large indigenous snare drums called *cajas* (Figure 1.8, CD track 7). Besides the different number of

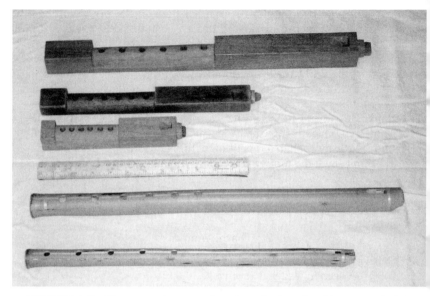

FIGURE 1.7   *From* top *to* bottom: *three sizes of* tarkas *played in consort, six-hole* pinkillu, *five-hole* pinkillu. *All are duct flutes.*

finger holes, six-hole *pinkillus* are slightly larger cane flutes pitched lower than the five-hole variant.

In Conima, lower pitch and slower tempi are associated with deeper or more serious feelings and contexts whereas higher pitch and faster tempi are associated with lighter or happy emotions. Within the same community and festival of *Candelaria* (February 1–2), six-hole *pinkillus* are used to accompany the most sacred or serious portions of this celebration for the first agricultural products; five-hole *pinkillus* are used to accompany courting dances and social dancing. In addition to Candelaria, in Conima, six-hole *pinkillus* are used for *Año Nuevo* (New Year's) to mark the transfer of political leadership in the *ayllus* and for certain events during the carnival season. Five-hole *pinkillus* are used for social dancing during Carnival, for roof-raising parties, and *Todos los Santos*.

Tarkas are duct flutes carved from wood. In ensemble, they are played in two or three sizes tuned in parallel octaves (if three sizes are used) and fourths or fifths. The mouthpieces of these instruments are constructed so that they easily split the octave, creating a buzzy, fat sound;

FIGURE 1.8 *Five-hole* pinkillu *ensemble with* caja *drums from the community of Japisi, Conima, performing for the Candelaria festival.*

a Peruvian friend called them "the Andean saxophone." *Tarkas* are a relatively recent arrival in Conima, coming from Bolivia during the first half of the twentieth century. They are only used for social dancing during Carnival (Figure 1.9, CD track 1) and, by the 1980s, had become so popular for this event that the majority of communities chose to play *tarkas* rather than five-hole *pinkillus*, the other option during Carnival for social dancing.

During the first half of the twentieth century, several other indigenous instruments were played in Conima which have gone out of use. There were two types of single-row panpipes. Certain communities played *chokelas* for Corpus Christi. *Chokelas* are large end-notched vertical flutes of pre-Columbian origin that resemble the smaller *kena*, or *quena*, used widely in the Andes and among 'folkloric' ensembles throughout the world. *Chokelas* and similar end-notched vertical flutes with different names (e.g., *kena*) are still regularly played by indigenous musicians in Huancané and other parts of Peru and Bolivia (Figure 1.10).

FIGURE 1.9 *Tarkas de Putina performing for dancing in the plaza of Conima during Carnival.*

In addition, brass bands are hired by *vecinos* for certain festivals in Conima. Growing in importance during the nineteenth century, brass bands are one of the most important types of ensembles for fiesta dancing and processions throughout the Andes. They are favored for their loud volume and adaptability for playing a wide variety of genres (see Chapter 3). It is striking that stringed instruments, so important elsewhere in the Andes, have not been adopted by indigenous musicians in Conima.

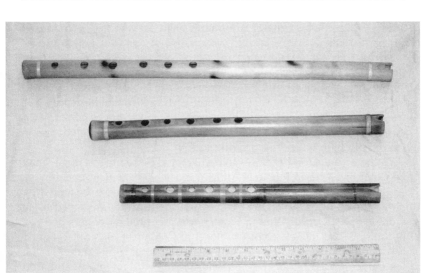

FIGURE 1.10 *End-notched flutes of pre-Columbian origin. The larger two are known by various local names such as* chokela; *the smallest is generally known as* kena.

The night before most festivals in Conima, the core musicians of a given indigenous community ensemble come together to collectively compose between one and three new tunes for that year's event. They do so within the established characteristics of a given genre which limit, and thus guide, the compositional process. As shown earlier, the vast majority of music composed by *ayllu* musicians is in AABBCC form, with a good deal of motivic repetition between the major sections and with the use of stock genre formulas (like the *chuta chuta* figure for the *siku ligero* and *choclo* genres). The placement of the formulas is also standard. Thus, in the *ligero* genre, the *chuta* figure (**ch**) occurs as follows: A**ch**, A**ch**, B**ch**, B, C, C**ch** (CD tracks 3 and 4). The long-held chords at the cadences of *lento* sections fall in the same places (CD track 2). The C sections tend to be the shortest and basically function as quick codas using motives that occurred in earlier sections. Within a given section for most genres, the melodies descend or have an undulating shape, with arch-shaped melodies being the main exception.

There is a common idea that most Andean music is *pentatonic* (five pitches in the scale). In fact, throughout the Andes a variety of scales are used, and this is true for Conima as well. *Tarka* music is composed primarily using the pentatonic scale; five-hole *pinkillu* music uses a variety of six-tone scales; and music played on *sikus* uses a variety of six- and seven-tone scales. Most music in Conima is composed in simple binary meter, but the rhythmic feel produced by the drums and syncopated melodies varies for the different instrumental genres. For example, the bass and snare drummers accompanying *tarka* and *pitu* ensembles model their rhythmic patterns on the specific melody being played but tend to provide a swing feel.

Some of the sound features that characterize Conimeño music may be generalized for indigenous Andean music more widely. Indigenous Andeans value high-pitched melodic ranges. Flutes tend to be forcefully blown to produce the higher octave, and instruments are tuned high; women and especially young women are preferred as singers because of their natural ranges. Another aspect of Conimeño musical style that can be generalized for other Andean indigenous communities is the long, open-ended performance of short forms with intensive repetition of motives and the use of sequences within a given piece. As in minimalist music more broadly, where slight changes can have a dramatic effect against a backdrop of repetition, indigenous Andean musicians are finely attuned to slight variations in tempi, the pitch levels of consorts, and subtle details of performance that they recognize as distinguishing one community ensemble from another within the district. For indigenous Andean musicians, slight variations provide major contrasts within genres and traditions that appear homogenous to outsiders; they also tend to eschew the obvious or dramatic contrasts that are favored in many cosmopolitan musics (see Chapter 5).

In Conima as in other indigenous Andean communities, instrumental and vocal *timbres* (quality of sound) are dense. The forceful (overblowing) of flutes creates a breathy quality and abundant overtones for a dense timbre (compared to the thinner timbres favored in cosmopolitan classical music). Panpipes are often constructed with a resonating row an octave above the main *ira* and *arca* rows; the air that spills over into the resonating rows adds additional sound and density (Figure 1.11). Moreover, the octave pitches are tuned purposefully wide so that the overtones do not match up precisely, creating complex combination tones (variety of overtones) that provide a dense sound. Likewise, the men who make consorts of panpipes purposefully tune them "wide" (slight variances among unison and octave pitches) to create a rich, dense tone quality. I already mentioned that some *pinkillu* players purposefully play slightly higher or lower than the median pitch line to

FIGURE 1.11 *Partners interlocking their* ira *and* arca siku *parts. Note the octave resonator row attached to each panpipe.*

the same effect, and *tarkas* are constructed so that forceful blowing will *split the octave* (hover between the lower and higher octaves on a given pitch) to create a dense, buzzy sound. Whereas the *pinkillu, pitu,* and other Aymara examples on the CD may seem slightly out of tune to North American listeners, the sound of wide tuning is precisely what Conimeños have grown up with and like to hear. Different tuning systems are the result of early socialization and are part of what makes individual musical traditions unique.

In Chapter 5, when describing the cosmopolitan form of 'folkloric Andean music,' I emphasize that while urban middle-class performers may play indigenous instruments and tunes, they do so using cosmopolitan tuning, textures, and timbres because of their own socialization in a different cultural formation and soundscape. They also usually perform in presentational contexts for audiences rather than in fully participatory settings, as in Conima. It is this deeper level of musical values that distinguishes indigenous lifeways from those of local *mestizos* as well as from people in the cosmopolitan formation. Identities and cultural positions are not simply costumes that can be put on and taken off at will (donning a poncho, playing a panpipe). They are also based in the deep-seated habits of thought, value, and practice that articulate, and are the result of, particular environments, experiences, and socialization. The close coherence between participatory music making as a type of practice and the egalitarian ethics in Aymara communities is a case in point.

PARTICIPATORY MUSIC MAKING IN CONIMA

It was during my time in Conima that I began to glimpse how different cultural conceptions could be regarding the very idea of what *music* is. One time a North American fiddler friend visited me while I was living with the family of my friend and teacher Filiberto Calderón. One morning Filiberto asked where Ralph was and I told him that he was back in our room playing the fiddle. Filiberto immediately queried "Who is he playing with?" I responded that he was simply playing by himself. Filiberto shot me a look of disbelief and asked "Why would he want to do that!?" It seemed outside his frame of comprehension.

In Conima, music making is strictly a collective social activity that takes place in public community and districtwide festivals. During my two years there, I never encountered anyone playing music alone; and from Filiberto's reaction to Ralph, it seemed to be considered aberrant behavior. Conima is radical in this regard; elsewhere in Peru, indigenous people play music alone for their own enjoyment. For example, in the neighboring Department of Cusco, I encountered young boys playing *charango* or *kena* alone for entertainment while pasturing their families' animals. In Conima, even practicing or learning music alone is rare, although men sometimes softly compose new tunes on an instrument alone at home in anticipation of an upcoming festival.

In Conimeño conception, music is more than just the sounds that are made; it is a combination of sound, motion of the dance, and highly stylized social interaction in festival events. Dance is so integral to the notion of musical performance that flute or panpipe musicians refer to their performance activities as dancing. Indeed, during performance, instrumentalists walk in one or more concentric circles (an activity they call dancing). But more importantly, dance is the most inclusive fiesta performance activity that potentially involves all the men, women, boys, and girls of a community, who move in concentric circles around the instrumentalists—either as couples or in a single line—doing a simple shuffle step. Music *is* dancing and is *for* dancing.

Music (hereafter to be understood as sound/motion/social interaction) in Conima is participatory at its core, although performance roles are determined by gender. *Participatory music* is defined here as a particular type of music making in which there are no artist–audience distinctions, only participants and potential participants. Moreover, in this type of tradition, the quality of a performance is judged by the level of participation and the practices and style of the music are oriented toward inspiring maximum participation. Participatory music is for *doing* rather than *listening*.

In highly developed participatory traditions, such as those in Conima, there is a place for beginners as well as experts. People with different levels of musical investment and skill perform together, and this practice is itself important for learning as well as comfort. Since beginners, intermediate players, and experts all perform together, people a step above provide accessible models for learning. Participatory traditions usually include a variety of roles such that people at any skill level can find a balance between their abilities and the degree of challenge necessary to keep them engaged: if all roles were simple, experienced musicians would become bored; if all were difficult, neophytes would become discouraged. These characteristics apply precisely to much of the music making in Conima as well as to participatory traditions in various parts of the world.

These features also contrast with *presentational* musical performance, in which clear artist–audience distinctions are made. In presentational performance, the artists have a responsibility to entertain an audience that is not directly participating in music making and dance, and this responsibility gives rise to a different set of style characteristics and practices. For example, in presentational ensembles, the members tend to be at a similar skill level and personnel are often chosen on the basis of musical ability. In presentational performance, textures and timbres tend to be more transparent so that listeners can follow what is happening musically. Contrasts of various types are preplanned to keep listening audiences interested, and virtuosity and solos are included for the same reason.

In Conima, men may perform as instrumentalists, dancers, or singers as they choose. As in most indigenous communities in the Andes, instrumental performance is strictly considered a male domain while women participate as singers and dancers (there are exceptions, such as women playing a small drum known as *tinya* in central Peru and certain female flute traditions in Bolivia). Many daily tasks in Conima are determined by gender, and gendered performance roles fit this general pattern. When I asked women in Conima if they would like to play instruments, the typical response was surprise: "Why would I want to do that? That is for the men." The situation is akin to wearing pants and dresses in the United States. While women can choose to wear either pants or dresses, it never occurs to me to put on a dress—"That is something only women do; why would I want to wear a dress?"

Gendered roles notwithstanding, any male is welcome to play an instrument in his community ensemble and any male or female is welcome to dance. There is actually some social pressure for people to participate, especially for districtwide festivals in the town plaza, since the larger the group, the stronger the showing. In addition, because of the egalitarian ethos and conflict-avoidance style guiding social life, no one, regardless of skill level, is discouraged from participating, and even inadequate performance or playing an instrument that is out of tune with the rest of the ensemble is not (publicly) commented on or overtly noticed.

These social practices do not suggest that the quality of performance is not important to Conimeños. As already suggested, performance in the districtwide festivals is the main way communities publicly represent themselves to others, and it is the main way that they fortify bonds within their own communities. Quality of performance is important, but "quality" does not simply involve abstracted musical sound and choreography. Quality is equally judged by how many people participate—to make a strong showing in the town plaza and to index community unity and investment at home—and by the social interaction within the performance itself. In places like Conima, where participatory music is the mainstay, music making and dance are media for heightened social interaction, the strengthening of relationships, and fun; they are social *activities* and means to these ends, not *art forms* and ends in themselves.

The musical situation in Conima could be compared to a neighborhood softball game in the United States when people come together to play for fun and friendship. Within the ranks of the players, there are some people who are deeply invested in softball and through repeated practice are good at it; others might be lousy players but join in to do something with their friends. Everyone who shows up is usually allowed to play—who is going to tell a friend that he is not good enough? The more competitive ones in the bunch might groan inwardly when a teammate flubs an easy fly but, if they have any class, will offer encouragement, make a joke, or say nothing. The "quality" of the game is ultimately judged by how much fun participants had playing, which in turn depends on the quality of social interaction while playing—the "bad sport" who makes his teammates feel badly about themselves does more damage than good to the game, even if he is a flawless pitcher and hitter. Such is the case within community ensembles in Conima; to tell an out-of-tune flute player to go away would do more damage to the music than the sound of the out-of-tune flute itself.

If no one can pitch, hit, or catch at all, the game goes nowhere and becomes boring. The players who have skill carry the game and make it fun for everyone. This is also true of participatory music traditions. In Conima, each community has a group of men who are deeply invested in instrumental performance and consequently have developed advanced performance and perhaps compositional skills. Conimeños I spoke with on the matter do not believe in innate musical talent. Rather, they feel that musical ability is the result of enthusiasm and musical experience—people who put their heart into music making and do it a lot gain skill.

Within the ranks of the self-selected core musicians, several usually stand out as *guías*, or guides. *Guías* are informal leaders of an ensemble. Other participants look to these men for guidance because they can recall and initiate a large number of tunes, have a good sense of tempo, and are strong players who others will be able to follow clearly. Due to the egalitarian social style in Conima, *guías* also have to have certain personal qualities. They have to lead gently and modestly through example and allow others to continually choose them to lead. I once witnessed a *guía* become overbearing with his ensemble mates: they quickly began to ignore him, and someone else soon stepped into his role. While a dictatorial conductor or strict bandleader might be effective at getting the best sound out of her ensemble for a presentational performance, Conimeños do not respond well to such hierarchical relations; they tend to avoid *vecinos* when they can, and they simply ignore people of their communities who become too assertive, which is considered rude behavior.

While the participation of *guías* and core musicians and dancers is inspired by their own passion for performance, others take part for a variety of reasons. Some join in simply to be social, to support the community, and to have fun. Some men are attracted by the fact that fiesta sponsors usually provide extra food, drink, and coca leaves for the instrumentalists who form the bedrock of the event. People participate in different roles (dancing, playing, drinking, socializing) and may switch roles during a long festival. Instrumentalists outside the musical core usually learn the newly composed pieces and, in fact, basic instrumental skills by playing during festivals. People's ability to learn during actual performances is facilitated by the fact that they have all grown up with this music as well as by the nature of the music itself. The strict AABBCC structure, the use of genre-specific formulas, the high degree of motivic repetition between sections, the constantly repeated rhythms, and the long performances of a given piece make Conimeño music easy to learn.

Like musical behavior, Conimeño musical sound is strongly guided by the broader ethical system. An often-stated musical value is that ensembles should "play as one" or "sound like one instrument" and that there should be no 'holes' (rests, silences) in a group's sound. These ideas refer to the dense textures of the wind ensembles involving the wide tuning and dense timbres already described, the large size of the ensembles, as well as a good deal of overlapping of parts. Melodies tend to be played in heterophony or, to use Steven Feld's (1988) phrase, "in-sync-and-out-of-phase." That is, rhythmic attacks and durations of given melodic pitches vary slightly (out of phase), which creates multiple subtly overlapped lines, all of which are oriented to the same rhythmic groove (in sync). Panpipe players hold their pitches over the beginnings of their partners' pitches, creating another type of overlap.

The dense textures and loud volume of Conimeño wind ensembles, or what I like to call the "wall of sound approach," can be understood in various ways. First, these sonic characteristics serve a kind of *cloaking function* common to participatory musics generally. The dense, overlapping textures and loud dynamics "cover" the contributions of less secure players, who can join in without fear that the mistakes they make will stand out. Thus, these sonic characteristics actually help inspire full participation. The densely meshed sound of the wind ensembles also stems from and articulates the general Conimeño trait that individuals do not like to stand out in public settings and that the collective is emphasized above the individual. People told me that it is a sign of bad playing if one's panpipe or flute pitches "escape" (stand out) from the overall mesh of sound. When an ensemble is playing well, the overall effect is a sonic portrait of the group itself: a well-integrated egalitarian collective in which individualism is downplayed. This is somewhat circular, however, in that good performance (as Conimeños define it) is the result of strong community spirit and egalitarian ethos. Thus, the musical *signs* (perceivable sounds) that represent the nature of Conimeño communities are the direct result of the very ethical disposi- tions and social integration that the signs stand for.

In keeping with Conimeño attitudes that emphasize the collec- tive over the individual, there are no places for highlighted solos in Conimeño wind music; everyone simply plays (a variant of) the melody repeatedly as loudly as possible. Although there are no soloists, there are certain performance techniques that add to the overall density and allow advanced players to challenge themselves while playing the for- mulaic melodies that are accessible to less skilled instrumentalists. In a technique called *requinteando* for panpipe performance, skilled *ira*-row players improvise harmonic or counter lines simultaneously with their *arca*-row partners' pitches and vice versa. There are multiple counter lines that can be invented in these spaces which provide continuing interest for experts, but as with all wind performance, the goal is to play these improvised parts so that they blend with the overall ensemble sound and do not stand out.

One of the first principles of organizing a presentational perfor- mance is that different types of variety and contrast must be pro- grammed to hold the audience's attention. Participatory music, on the other hand, emphasizes repetition, "sameness," of instrumental timbres (wind instruments are not mixed in ensembles) and of genres, rhythms, and tempos (one or two may be played continuously throughout a three-day festival). Most important to the function of participatory music, the same rhythmic grooves and tempi are re- peated, piece to piece, throughout multiday fiestas so that community members can get in sync with each other and stay in sync playing and dancing.

Much of the social power and aesthetic fulfillment of participatory music come through synchrony of sound and movement—moving and sounding "as one" within long performances of a single rhythmic groove. Anthropologist Edward Hall suggests that synchrony and similarity of gestures, movement, and body language are crucial signs, often perceived low in focal awareness, of social comfort and belonging in daily interactions (1977). In music/dance performance, these signs are brought to a higher level of focal awareness and are experienced directly, without verbal mediation, as true signs of similarity and, thus, identity. It is through rhythmic repetition and synchrony, what William McNeill calls "muscular bonding," that deep, unspoken, feelings of being as one are created; and this is why such performances actually function to bolster people's sense of community unity and identity (1995).

ACTIVITY 1.5 *Jot down a list of participatory activities that you have engaged in that created this sense of social synchrony and bonding with other people (e.g., singing in church, team sports, or physical work, among many others). Take a moment to remember what the different experiences felt like, and in a few sentences, analyze what made the experience memorable.*

FESTIVALS IN CONIMA

There are two major types of fiestas in the District of Conima: those which are performed on an annual basis and are connected to the agricultural cycle, the Catholic calendar, the political cycle, or some combination and variable life-cycle and work-related events such as weddings, first hair-cutting ceremonies for children, and roof raisings. In certain major festivals, such as Carnival, *Año Nuevo* (New Year's), and *Todos los Santos* (All Saints' Day), most communities celebrate. In other events such as *San Isidro* (May 14–15) and *Candelaria* (February 1–2), only certain indigenous communities have the custom of holding fiestas. On the average, a two- to three-day festival will be held somewhere in the district once a month, and major fiestas are often extended with three-day weddings, which are also community affairs. Here, I discuss two fiestas, *Año Nuevo* and *San Isidro*; descriptions of other Conimeño festivals can be found in my book *Moving Away from Silence* (1993).

Año Nuevo.   The fiesta of *Año Nuevo*, on the afternoon and evening of January 1, is related to the political *cargo* cycle. The role of serving as community headman, which every adult male ideally should pass through, is considered a difficult and troublesome responsibility as well as an honor. *Año Nuevo* is a fiesta for the outgoing headman in recognition of his service and a celebration by the man and his wife of their new freedom from that responsibility. The fiesta is celebrated by each of the indigenous communities, with the ex-headman serving as sponsor and host.

In 1986, community members began to arrive at the home of the outgoing headman about mid-day. Benches were arranged outside the house on the patio and in a large room inside, where the visiting men took seats and conversed quietly. The women and children formed a separate circle on the ground or floor somewhat away from the men. The social separation of men and women in public settings is typical; even in weddings the groom spends most of his time with the men and the bride, with the women. Dancing provides the main activity where men and women interact closely in public. After a critical mass appeared, the hosts served a meal of soup and *segunda* (second course) to all. Food is the most important demonstration of hospitality in Conima, and *segundas* including meat, potatoes, and vegetables are especially enjoyed during festivals since meat is not a common part of the daily diet. Drinking is also largely reserved for public fiestas, and the host serves grain alcohol or, if he is able, commercial beer, which is particularly prized (Figure 1.12). Drinking takes place using one glass that is passed person to person within the male and female circles. Before drinking, each individual offers a few drops to the Earth with words of thanks and to other local spiritual forces.

After the meal is concluded, the host and other community elders enact a *t'inka*, a ritual to maintain active reciprocal relations with the Earth, local spiritual forces, and other community members. *T'inka* rituals are performed at various key times during fiestas, before a musical rehearsal begins, and for any solemn occasion. A woven cloth is laid on the ground or a table and a pile of coca leaves is placed in the center, encircled by cigarettes and two cups of alcohol, one on either side (Figure 1.13). Chewed with a lime substance to activate the leaves, coca is a mild stimulant (somewhat like coffee but without the caffeine buzz) used by indigenous Andeans to provide energy while working and to ward off hunger. Coca is also a very important ritual item in indigenous communities on social occasions and, most formally, in the *t'inka*.

FIGURE 1.12   *Men sharing food and drinking beer at a private home in* ayllu *Sulcata during a festival. The woven bags the men are holding are used to carry coca leaves.*

With the host and elders leading the ritual, people select three perfect coca leaves from the pile and place them in the cups with whispered words to the spiritual forces to whom the cups will be offered. This operation is done three times for different divinities. The first pair of cups with alcohol and coca are thrown into the air, one for *Condor Mamani* (a divinity of the home and family), and one in the direction of the place of spiritual power on the family's land. The second pair of cups are offered to the community's *achachila* (a divinity associated with a particular mountain, also translated as 'place'), and to the *aviadores* (powerful forces like *achachilas* but not place-bound). The third pair are offered to *Pachamama* (concept of the living female Earth) and to the ancestors. After this has been concluded, all the remaining adults pick three 'perfect' coca leaves and, lining them up, offer them to someone who is near them or with whom they wish to express a particular bond as a kind of social communion; then, those who wish to can take cigarettes. It is through this ritual that direct communication takes place between community members and the spiritual forces that so directly affect their lives.

FIGURE 1.13 *Setting up for a* t'inka *ritual.*

Mid-afternoon, while the guests are drinking and talking, the men of the community who own six-hole *pinkillus* and know the *Año Nuevo* music begin to take out their flutes from under their ponchos or jackets. Other men go home to get their flutes and *cajas* (large indigenous snare drums), while the others begin warming up (Figure 1.14). For the 1986 fiesta of the community of central Sulcata, no rehearsal was held the night before and atypically no new pieces were composed, so the musicians began to play through pieces from preexisting years. When enough instrumentalists had assembled, they formed a circle outside

FIGURE 1.14 *Six-hole* pinkillu *and* caja *ensemble at the home of the outgoing headman,* Año Nuevo.

the house and began to play in earnest. The music drew more musicians and visitors, and the ensemble grew from five to fifteen flute players accompanied by *cajas* and a bass drum. Gradually, people got up to dance in a circle around the musicians.

The dance, which in this context is simply called *"Año Nuevo,"* is actually the same in style and form as the dance done in many festivals. Couples form a double circle (the men on the inside) dancing counterclockwise around the ensemble. The men and women hold both of their partner's hands (left hand holds the partner's right) at waist level between their bodies, and they move forward either doing a quick shuffle step or the *wayno*, which is comprised of an alternating step on the ball of the right foot (knee slightly bent) and the left foot placed flat. Usually at the end of a musical section, the end of each repetition of the form, or at will, the man will turn the woman under his right arm, releasing her other hand. Sometimes all the dancers will join hands, men and women alternating, and dance in a ring around the musicians. The musicians may perform in a stationary circle, but they also often dance by moving in a natural walk in the opposite direction of the dancers.

After a period of dancing at the outgoing headman's house, everyone gets ready to leave for the plaza of the district capital town of Conima. Playing as they go, they begin their journey; couples who want to dance form two columns moving out in front of the instrumentalists and then doubling back. As honored members of the party, the ex-headman and his wife usually dance at the head of the columns and serve as *guías* of the dance. Upon reaching the plaza, they stop to rest, drink, and re-group. They then enter and circle the plaza playing and dancing, ending up in their customary performance spot in the plaza, surrounded by the music/dance ensembles from other communities. People who do not yet wish to play or dance stand with their community, and in the early hours of the plaza celebration, each community group performs and socializes separately from the other groups.

All afternoon, the ensembles alternate periods of dancing with times for drinking and resting. In fiestas such as *Año Nuevo* and *Carnivales*, where there are many ensembles located right next to each other in the plaza (circa 50 yards square), the different ensembles usually time their rest periods so as to alternate performances with the groups on either side. As the afternoon wears on, crowds of spectators from town and other communities begin to form around the groups that have the best dancers and music. When a particular ensemble begins to draw a crowd, it tends to play longer and louder, select the best pieces, and often starts playing at the same time as the neighboring ensembles in order to hold their audience.

It is at these times when competition between communities becomes the most obvious. For example, the community of Central Sulcata customarily sets up right next to the community of Huata. These two groups resulted from a split within a single *ayllu*, and thus, there was a particular rivalry between them. They were also considered two of the best music/dance ensembles and often drew a crowd to that corner of the plaza. For *Año Nuevo*, as the afternoon wore on and the celebration heated up with drink and animation, these two groups started playing simultaneously, seeing who could play loudest and longest, and more community members joined in dancing to strengthen their showing. As the action escalated, people from town or from communities that did not send ensembles to town began to gather in greater numbers and, as the drink and spirit moved them, joined in dancing with the ensemble of their choice.

This type of informal musical competition is standard for most districtwide fiestas in Conima, and it is a feature of festival performance in many parts of the Andes. There are no official judges or prizes. 'Winning the day' is gauged on the basis of the groups that created the most excitement, animation, and interaction—the greatest "buzz." Small community groups do not draw much attention; but in major festivals, usually there are two to four ensembles that make a splash in different parts of the plaza, and the members of each typically claim that 'they won' or 'were the best' at that year's event. In fact, many groups go home feeling, or at least saying, that they were the winners; such is the nature of competition within this egalitarian setting.

Things can get a bit wild by late afternoon. The dancing grows in intensity; the music gets louder and more raucous. If a personal feud has been brewing during past months, it may erupt in a fistfight at such times. During one fiesta, someone from another community came over and kicked in a drum of the group I was playing with. No one ever understood the reason, but it almost resulted in a battle between the two ensembles. People also begin to move about more freely, drinking and talking with friends and relatives from other communities, and the divisions between community units begin to break down. Districtwide fiestas celebrated in the plaza generally have this form of escalating intensity and animation, and at their height they provide an incredible contrast with the quietude and solemnity of daily life.

For *Año Nuevo* 1986, groups who lived far away from town began to leave around dusk so as to be home before dark. The more enthusiastic ensembles stayed on, and those who had a reputation to uphold attempted to be the last to leave, each ensemble taking a turn around the plaza before heading out of town. Most groups played and danced all the way back to their homes. Men and women who did not wish the fiesta to end, slipped away with friends to continue drinking. As the sound of the *pinkillu* music finally faded in the night, only the hard-core revelers and those unable to walk remained behind.

San Isidro (May 14-15).   In Conima, the *Fiesta de San Isidro*, patron saint of agriculturalists, is often simply called *satiri*, the Aymara word for "planter of potatoes." As in many parts of the Andes, the names and significance of Catholic fiestas are often combined with, or supplanted by, local indigenous meaning. For example, in Conima, the festival of the Virgin of *Candelaria* is Catholic in name only; the fiesta comprises a series of dances and rituals for the first agricultural products of the year, and the saint is not even mentioned. Beginning in the 1500s, the Catholic Church superimposed its feast days on indigenous celebrations as part of the conversion process, the result being a blending of indigenous and Catholic beliefs and practices that is still evident today.

The fiesta of *San Isidro* in Conima illustrates this religious syncretism. On May 14, a small procession for the saint takes place; and on May 15, a mass is held in the church in the central plaza of the town. Neither is accompanied by music, and both are sparsely attended, primarily by *vecinos*. The people of certain *ayllus* celebrate this fiesta by performing a single dance drama known as *satiri*. *Dance dramas*, performed in festivals throughout Latin America, are costumed dances that present characters and themes of local history and significance (see Chapter 3). *San Isidro* is celebrated after the harvest and is a harvest celebration; in *satiri*, Conimeños enact their entire agricultural cycle. In 1985, three communities—Huata, Cambria, and Central Sulcata—celebrated the festival by dancing *satiri* accompanied by *sikus* (panpipes). Here, I will describe the event with special emphasis on the group from Sulcata, the community I was affiliated with.

Two days before the festival, a 'rehearsal' was held at the home of the fiesta sponsor in Sulcata. Only the core musicians attended this event that marks the real beginning of the festival. After a *t'inka* ritual was held and a meal served to the musicians, the evening was spent composing a new *satiri* march and playing through pieces composed in past years. Each community has its own unique repertory of pieces collectively composed by community members for any given genre. It is a point of community pride to compose at least one new piece for any given festival so that the community has something new to offer. The newly composed piece(s) is typically played more than any other during the festival it was composed for and thus becomes a kind of emblem or index for the community during that and subsequent years. *Satiri* involves two different panpipe genres, marches and dance pieces. *Satiri* music differs from the *siku lento* and *ligero* genres (but is like *imillani*) in that it is composed in the major mode (CD track 8).

Pieces are composed collectively in a kind of musical "brainstorming" session. Sitting in a circle, the core musicians softly blow motives or sections of pieces simultaneously as they think of them. Musical ideas that do not seem promising are simply ignored. If someone comes up with an interesting musical idea, others will listen and gradually join in playing it. At this point, if the original idea does not seem to have promise, individuals gradually stop playing it and go back to square one, riffing new ideas. If the motive or section still seems promising, the group will then brainstorm the next section of the AABBCC form based on this germinal idea. After an entire tune has been roughed out—by adding the additional sections bit by bit, playing them together, deciding whether they work, and brainstorming new ideas for portions not deemed attractive—group members will fine-tune the piece by suggesting small changes here and there and then playing through the piece with the new alterations. What was miraculous to me was that this whole process took place with hardly any discussion or even words being said. New ideas are offered simply by playing them, and others either accept them by joining in with the originator or reject them by ignoring them. Thus, there is no pointed or verbal rejection of anyone's musical suggestions; likewise, there is no particular recognition of individual contributions. By the end of the composition process, the input of a number of people is combined into a finished piece and 'the community' is considered the composer. Interestingly, group consensus decision making proceeds in much the same manner: verbal ideas are either simply ignored or repeated by new speakers, perhaps with modifications or additions, until the contributions of a number of people are combined into a finished decision that the community fashions together.

In the 1985 fiesta, Central Sulcata performed the *satiri* dance three times, accompanied by the panpipe ensemble, at the home of the fiesta sponsor within the community on the evening of May 14 and the morning of May 15. On the afternoon of the second day, the three communities came to town to perform simultaneously in their usual performance spots in the town plaza. In *satiri*, male dancers wear costumes including long black coats, knit masks, and funny hats. They also carry small replicas of the digging sticks used in agricultural work. Some men dress as women, and one person dresses up as a policeman complete with a wooden machine gun (Figure 1.15).

The dance sequence begins with an enactment of the redistribution of land. With a good deal of clowning, several dancers stretch a string across the performance space at different angles to indicate the marking

FIGURE 1.15 Satiri *dancers. Notice the toy digging sticks some of the dancers hold over their shoulders and the potatoes and corn "planted" on the ground in the dance space. The dancer taking the role of policeman may be seen in the background.*

off of land. Inevitably, land squabbles ensue and people engage in mock fighting. The policeman-dancer enters the fray in an attempt to bring peace, at which point everyone closes ranks, showering this figure of "outside authority" with blows and abuse. The second sequence of the dance is an enactment of planting. The male characters move backward pretending to make seed holes with their digging sticks, while the female characters lay actual products such as potatoes and corn in lines across the performance space. Following planting, the dancers stop for a simulated communal lunch break, the food being served on a *manta* (woven cloth) on the ground. After lunch, the *t'inka* ritual is comically performed. Two wooden cups are placed on a *manta* piled high with coca leaves. The dancers grab handfuls of coca and throw it around in the air, and the cups of alcohol are thrown at bystanders, while others roughly shove handfuls of leaves into the mouths of their fellow dancers. Community members watching the dancers found this parody of their most sacred ritual particularly hilarious.

Next comes the enactment of the cleaning of the fields, during which any rocks, sticks, or garbage found within the performance space are picked up by the dancers and hurled at bystanders. Then, the potatoes are hilled, and it is time for the dramatization of the *Candelaria* festival. The panpipe music ceases, and one or more dancers start blowing *Candelaria* music on *pinkillus* (CD track 7), while others gather up a few products in *mantas* and parade around the performance space with flags in an exaggerated manner. *Carnivales* follows close behind, and the *pinkillus* are again played for humorous parodies of carnival dancing. Then comes an enactment of the "Easter" fiesta, and the panpipe ensemble plays a *choclo* (CD track 4) piece associated with that event for the clowning *satiri* dancers. The final two segments of the dance drama include the harvest, in which the products laid out across the performance space are gathered up in *mantas* for the *pachamanka* (festive cooking of potatoes). For the *pachamanka*, real fires are set with straw and the dancers clown around, throwing "hot" potatoes back and forth. After the dance drama sequence has been completed, the *siku* ensemble continues to play and people continue to fool around, socialize, and drink.

As a dramatic enactment of the agricultural cycle, *satiri* has many points of interest. For example, while by the 1980s families typically worked the same lands year after year, land is formally owned by the community as a whole (in the past it may have been redistributed on a yearly basis). The attitudes expressed in the performance toward the policeman—a figure of outside authority stationed in the district by the state—are quite literal. The fact that the *Candelaria*, Carnival, and Easter festivals were all depicted within the context of the agricultural cycle is significant in suggesting that these Catholic holidays are really conceptualized locally in relation to indigenous agricultural rituals. It is also significant that this dramatization follows right after harvest time. It is as if the performance itself were a punctuation point, summing up the preceding cycle before beginning the next one.

Upon seeing *satiri* performed for the first time after having witnessed the life and customs in Conima, I was confused. It seemed that the entire performance was a satire by Conimeño peasants of themselves and the most important and sacred aspects of their lives; most striking was the ruthless parody of the *t'inka* ritual, in which dancers roughly shoved fistfuls of coca leaves into each others mouths instead of the delicate offering of three perfect leaves. I asked people about this impression, and they were surprised. I was assured that the performance was simply an enactment of the agricultural cycle with a serious and straightforward meaning. When I mentioned the humorous portrayal of the *t'inka*, my friends just shrugged and said the dancers were just joking around but that this did not affect the overall meaning.

Satiri is a serious self-portrait of Conimeño life through music and dance. Performed annually, it embodies and reminds of customs past and present and it encapsulates vital relations between the different parts of the annual cycle. *Satiri* is also a festival dance performed for the fun of dancers and onlookers. The wilder the antics became, the more fun people had. The desire to entertain onlookers in this semipresentational dance drama inspired the performers to greater hilarity. (It is semipresentational in that anyone who wanted to could perform but a number of people didn't and so became a kind of audience.) None of the Conimeños I spoke with about the dance perceived any contradiction between performers' outrageous behavior and the serious themes embedded within the dance. As I was told in Conima on more than one occasion, "dances have to have many meanings; they cannot only have one." In this case, the pragmatics of having a good time and the custom of enacting a serious self-portrait were simply two levels of meaning that, for Conimeños, easily and joyously coincide.

CHAPTER 2

Charango String Traditions

Before the arrival of the Spanish in the 1530s, stringed instruments were not played in the Andes, only drums, percussion, whistles, trumpets, and some of the winds described for Conima—panpipes, end-notched flutes, and transverse flutes. Europeans soon introduced stringed instruments such as the diatonic harp, violin, and guitar, as well as later instruments like the mandolin. They also introduced duct flutes (i.e., the recorder) and reed wind instruments. The stringed instruments were performed by *criollo* and *mestizo* musicians, but the harp and violin were quickly learned and adopted by indigenous people, who were initially trained by early colonial missionaries. The diatonic harp and violin are still important instruments for indigenous musicians in Ecuador and Peru and, to a much lesser extent, in Bolivia. The guitar and mandolin largely remained the domain of *criollo* and *mestizo* musicians until around the 1960s.

Instead, a new guitar variant known as *charango* emerged in the Andean region between Huancavelica, Peru, and Potosí, Bolivia, during the 1700s, its original area of diffusion following mining-trade routes. It was this instrument, rather than the guitar per se, that was adopted by indigenous musicians early on. Small in size, it was easily transportable, and the short string length allowed for the high-pitched sound favored by indigenous musicians. Since the concept *mestizo* suggests a blending of indigenous and European elements, the *charango* is *mestizo* in inception—it is modeled on the European guitar but altered in size to accommodate indigenous musical preferences. Nonetheless, until the 1920s the *charango* was associated with indigenous people or at least lower-class musicians. In the context of twentieth-century nationalist and regionalist movements known collectively as *indigenismo* ("Indianist" movement), higher-class *mestizos* and even large-*hacienda* owners, such as Andres Allencastre of Canas, Cusco, began to play the *charango*. The result was that by the 1970s, when I began researching this instrument, there were two distinct *charango* traditions—one *mestizo* and one indigenous—each cross-cut by a variety of regional *charango* styles.

A primary theme of this book involves the ways musical practices and style are both the result of and a means of communicating particular social identities and cultural positions. In this chapter, I compare the indigenous use of the *charango* in Canas, Cusco, with the *mestizo charango* style to illustrate the distinctive musical values and attitudes underlying these two *charango* traditions. That is, while we are dealing with one instrument, I believe that there are two separate approaches to the instrument defined by distinctive values, performance practices, contexts of performance, and sound style, all of which point to important differences in cultural orientation between indigenous people and *mestizos* in southern Peru. The comparison of indigenous Quechua and *mestizo charango* performance also underlines another prominent theme—the distinctive character of participatory and presentational music making. While it is true that indigenous and *mestizo* identities are somewhat fluid and situationally relative, the comparison of the two distinctive approaches to *charango* playing helps us identify the different cultural tendencies and sensibilities that characterize these two social groups. Framing the problem in this way brings up another important point.

Although stringed instruments came to the Andes with Europeans, some of them were adopted and adapted within indigenous lifeways and, through this process, became local indigenous instruments. This is clearly true for the *charango* but also for the harp and violin and, much later, the guitar and mandolin. Beginning in the 1500s, these local adoptions of foreign technologies provide early examples of what is currently referred to as "*cultural globalization*" and what I will discuss later in the book as *cosmopolitanism*. The example of the indigenous *charango* tradition suggests that it is often not the origin of a given technology, idea, or practice but rather its local use and meaning that is significant. The discussion of indigenous *charango* players in Canas also illustrates another theme of the book—the power of music to communicate across otherwise uncrossable barriers—in this case between adolescent lovers.

THE INDIGENOUS *CHARANGO*
OF CANAS, CUSCO

Several hundred miles to the north of Conima lies the Quechua-speaking province of Canas toward the southern tip of the Department of Cusco (see Figure 1.3). Located above the tree line, Canas is a desolate region of rolling hills and dispersed homesteads scattered around district capital towns populated by *vecinos*. The indigenous people of Canas raise livestock as well as potatoes and other tubers, the only crops that will grow at that altitude. They are part of what has been termed *qorilazo*, or horseman culture, of the high *puna* regions of southern Peru. Caneños practice common Andean customs of communal labor exchange and collective work projects and decision making, but they are typically more individualistic than the people of Quechua communities located in river valleys and strongly contrast with Conimeños in this regard.

Although not very far from Conima as the crow flies, Caneños perform totally different instruments, music, and dances from the Aymara of Conima. This illustrates the distinctiveness of localized musical traditions in the Andes—it would be as if the people of Connecticut and Massachusetts had totally different musical traditions. For rainy-season festivals, Caneños play long wooden vertical flutes known as *pinkullus*. Although a duct flute with a name similar to the Conimeño *pinkillu*, the *pinkullu* of Canas is really a different instrument—made of wood and four times the length of the Conimeño instrument (Figure 2.1). In Canas, *pinkullus* are performed solo or in groups of between two and six musicians without drum accompaniment. Because of their large size,

ACTIVITY 2.1   *Compare the sound of the Caneño* pinkullu *and the Conimeño* pinkillu *music heard on CD tracks 7, 9, and 11. In a few sentences, describe the differences of timbre, range, and "ensemble" texture; then describe some similarities that you can identify that might pertain to general Andean musical values and traits as described in the previous chapter.*

pinkullus are capable of producing low pitches, but they are consistently overblown to produce the greater volume, higher pitches, and dense, breathy sound generally favored by indigenous Andeans. Nonetheless, these instruments sound quite different from the *pinkillu* ensembles of Conima (CD tracks 9 and 11).

Pinkullus are used to accompany women's singing. As elsewhere in the Andes, indigenous women of Canas do not play instruments but, because of the general indigenous-Andean preference for high-pitched

FIGURE 2.1   Pinkullu *player in Canas, Cusco, dressed for Carnival.*

music, they are the favored singers. Unlike Conima but typical of Quechua communities, vocal music is central to most festival music traditions in Canas, and singing is also common in informal get-togethers in homes. The concluding high-pitched vocal ornament performed by Paulina Wilka at 00:24 on CD track 10 is typical of Peruvian Quechua singing. The *heterophonic* relationship between the *pinkullu* and vocal (performing variants of a single melody simultaneously) on CD track 11 is standard practice in Canas. In this performance, the variants of the melody are often so distinct that they sound like two different melodies weaving in and out of each other—almost like a beautiful sonic dance between the male instrumentalist and female singer. Reporting on an indigenous Quechua community in northern Potosí, Bolivia, Henry Stobart notes that

> Women do not play instruments, but are the principal singers and creators of song poetry. As such, they articulate a somewhat separate but complementary and interlocking sphere of musical knowledge.... The complementary nature of these gendered realms of musico-productive knowledge was sometimes made particularly explicit. For example, once when I recorded a young man singing to his own strummed *charango* accompaniment, he apologetically explained that the music was incomplete without a woman's voice. (2002:87–88)

Relationships of gender complementarity in music making are mirrored in other realms of social life, such as agricultural tasks, and in cosmological understandings of the world; for example, the Earth is considered a female principle and mountains are male.

Caneños play a variety of stringed instruments, in contrast to the Aymara of Huancané. Guitars and mandolins are used to play the *wayno* and other genres that have been widely popularized by radio since the 1960s (see Chapter 4). Some men have taken up the *bandurria*, an instrument shaped like a mandolin with sixteen to twenty strings divided into four *courses* (multiple strings fingered as one, as on a twelve-string guitar) and associated with the neighboring province of Canchis (Figure 2.2). These instruments are played by men in informal get-togethers and for self-entertainment rather than in public festival performance. Along with the wooden *pinkullu*, the other main musical instrument considered local and central to Caneño music making is the *charango*.

The *charango* is a small variant of the guitar that is unique to the Andes. A huge number of local instruments modeled on the Spanish guitar, or *vihuela*, but with varying sizes, numbers of strings, tunings, and names exist throughout Latin America. The Mexican and Chilean *guitarrones* are the largest of these (see the Sheehy book in this series), and the *charango* is the smallest. *Charangos* used by indigenous musicians vary in shape, size, materials, and numbers of strings depending on local preferences and the whims of specific makers. An extremely small five-stringed instrument is used in the Peruvian department of Ayacucho; there are also round and teardrop-shaped instruments made from gourds, armadillo

FIGURE 2.2   *Carnival dancing in the plaza of Tinta, province of Canchis, Cusco. The men play* bandurrias *to accompany the singing of their partners.*

shell, crocodile skin, or wood. There are even *charangos* made in the shape of mermaids! The most common types are flat-backed and round-backed wooden (or armadillo shell) instruments in the form of a small guitar (Figure 2.3). Most *charangos* have five courses of double strings, a common alternative being twelve-stringed instruments with two triple courses. Although regional tunings abound, a standard tuning is E-E, A-A, E-E, C-C, G-G, played as a kind of semi-open A minor/C major tuning.

I initially traveled to Canas in 1982 because I had heard that the *charango* was an important indigenous instrument in that region and that *charango* players commonly came into the district capital towns on market days with their instruments. I arrived in Descanso for the Saturday market; catching a truck into the region from the Vilcanota river valley far below was easiest on market days. Like Conima, the town of Descanso was centered around a large plaza. Sitting on the ground around the square, women and girls from local communities

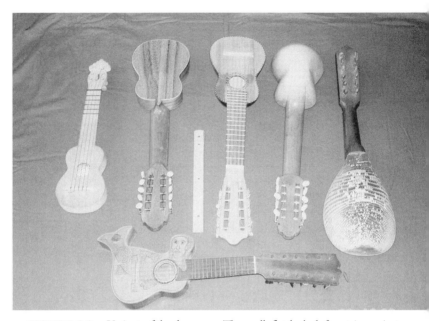

FIGURE 2.3 *Variants of the* charango. *The small, flat-backed, five-string variant on the left is an older type (late nineteenth to early twentieth century) from the Department of Ayacucho; note the five wooden frets on the fingerboard. Next to it is a ten-string, flat-backed* mestizo *charango from the city of Cusco with geared tuners, built in the 1980s. Moving right are two round-backed, ten-string* charangos *seen from the front and the back, a contemporary type most strongly associated with* mestizo *players of Bolivia and the type used by the cosmopolitan "folkloric" groups (see Chapter 5). Far right is a teardrop-shaped, twelve-string* charango *made with an armadillo shell sound box and wooden friction pegs (late 1970s). At the bottom is a flat-backed* charango *made in the shape of a mermaid with rough wooden friction pegs (late 1970s).*

and elsewhere were selling potatoes, meat, clothing, and other products. With a feeling that I had hit the mother lode for recording indigenous *charango* music, I also noticed five or six young men standing around in different parts of the plaza holding and sporadically playing their instruments (Figure 2.4). I especially noticed one extremely well-dressed young man whose instrument was ornately decorated with ribbons and mirrors (Figure 2.5). I approached him as he was entering the plaza and after some conversation was allowed to record the piece he was strumming—a tune, I was to learn later, known as

FIGURE 2.4 Charango *player in the Saturday market in Descanso, Canas, Cusco.*

the *tuta kashua* (night *kashua*, or night dance). I asked him if the tune had words, and he sang for my tape recorder (CD track 12). After a while, I approached another young man in another part of the plaza and found that he was strumming the same tune, as were all the others I approached that day. At my request, these boys would play one or two other tunes for me, but left to their own devices they returned to strumming the *tuta kashua* as surely as water finds its way downhill.

FIGURE 2.5 Charango *player comes a-courtin' in the Saturday market in Descanso, Canas. His festive hat and clothes are unique to Canas, and the instrument, highly decorated with ribbons and mirrors, indicates his seriousness of purpose.*

I must admit that I felt let down. I had traveled two days to get to Descanso from Cusco city, and these young musicians seemed to only want to play one tune!? So much for recording a rich repertory of indigenous *charango* music, I thought.

True to my quest, I stayed in Canas, traveling to other towns for their market days, but encountered the same situation. In the town of Langui, I approached a *charango* player who had a particularly forceful manner of playing the *tuta kashua*. Prompted by my questions, he told me that he lived in another area but had not had any luck there and so came to the Langui market hoping to do better. "Better at what?" I asked. "There is no one at home who will go with me to the *punchay kashua* (day dance)," he said sadly, clutching his *charango*. "I was hoping I could find a girl here." No luck here either, as it turned out.

Back in Descanso for the following Saturday and the Saturday after that, I began to notice that boys playing *charango* were hovering around a particular girl—nonchalantly strumming the *tuta kashua* tune somewhere in her vicinity, decked out in their best, *charangos* decked out too, little eye contact, cool guy. The girls were equally cool, looking down at the ground, off in the distance, or anywhere but (with the occasional slip) in the boys' direction—or, if they did, with looks of disinterest or boredom. It is not easy being an adolescent boy, or girl for that matter. This is where the *charango* and the *tuta kashua* song come in. With a few exceptions, only young unmarried men played the *charango* in Canas. In fact, the instrument was so strongly associated with courting that if a married man was seen walking around his village carrying one, people would joke that he was fooling around. For an unmarried boy, simply playing the instrument repeatedly near the girl of his heart on market days communicates his interest without having to say a thing.

There is a certain magic in the music used to attract a bride, but in southern Peru and Bolivia the magic of the *charango* is fortified by certain ritual practices involving the instrument and, amazingly enough, mermaids. In Canas, as elsewhere in this region, specific villages and towns are said to have their own mermaid (*sirena*) living in a river, spring, or lake nearby. Stobart reports that among Quechua communities in Potosí, Bolivia, *sirenas* are believed to be the sources of new musical compositions, and the tunes thus received serve as a bridge between the supernatural and human realms. In southern Peru, *sirenas* are considered to be seductresses with all the power and danger implied. When a boy obtains a *charango* to begin courting (either by buying or borrowing one from a friend or relative), he seeks to tap into this power through certain ritual practices. There are many local variants of these stories. In Canas, the boy takes his *charango* and places it on a woven cloth (*manta*) with coca leaves, sweets, and other offerings by the place where the *sirena* resides. He then leaves it there all night but does not stay himself. If he encountered the *sirena*, she might seduce him into the water and he would drown or he might go crazy or come to harm in other ways. When the boy returns in the morning, the *charango* is perfectly tuned and is now invested with the *sirena*'s power to seduce. In another variant from Puno, Peru, the boy twirls a lock of his beloved's hair with his own and places it inside the *charango*. He then leaves the instrument by the *sirena* overnight, and by morning the instrument will have the power to attract and hold the affections of the girl for life.

Once I began investigating the association of *charango* with courting, I was told many such stories; but I never saw anyone do these things. Beyond such extraordinary measures, simply playing the *charango* had the power to communicate a boy's intentions because the instrument was so strongly associated with courting. The meaning of this associative sign was strengthened by the *tuta kashua* tune itself, as we shall see. During the time of my research, the courting process in Canas had several discernable steps. The first was for a boy to obtain a *charango*, learn how to tune it, and gain the basic skills necessary to play the *kashua* tunes (*kashua* is a pre-Columbian Quechua name for circle dances). As is true for the wind traditions of Conima, *charango* playing in Canas is a *nonspecialist* tradition, meaning that it is relatively easy for anyone to gain the basic skills necessary to play—lucky for the boys who want to find a bride.

A key style trait that defines the indigenous *charango* tradition in Canas and elsewhere is that the instrument, with ten or twelve thin metal strings, is only strummed. Indigenous players place one, or at most two, fingers on the fret board at a time to strum a melody against the backdrop of multiple reverberating open strings. As opposed to playing fully formed chords, their approach to the instrument is melodic and thus parallels indigenous wind performance. The strumming of multiple, often slightly dissonant, open thin metal strings produces the same density of texture that was described for Conimeño wind ensembles and is in keeping with this general indigenous musical preference.

Indigenous *charango* players in Canas and elsewhere also prefer small flat-backed instruments tuned as high as possible without breaking the strings. I once traveled in Canas with a larger round-backed *mestizo charango* with nylon strings and a lower octave E string in the central course. Caneños expressed a dislike for the sound of my instrument, saying that it "did not sound like a *charango*," "it was too *ronco*" (rough, hoarse). They said that a *charango* "should cry out like a cat." An alternative local name for the instrument, *chillador*, expresses this same aesthetic preference for a bright, high-pitched sound—*chillar* means to scream, to shriek.

The *tuta kashua* tune that the boys learn and play all day at the market is comprised of two short melodic phrases corresponding to the vocal melody and lasting three beats each. The two phrases are distinguished only by different endings on a higher **(h)** and lower **(l)** pitch, which can be ordered in different ways; the piece thus involves the same intensive repetition of melodic material as described for Conimeño wind music. As with minimalist music in general, indigenous Andeans recognize 'small' differences as making pronounced differences against a backdrop of intensive repetition; thus, Raul Quispe provides variation simply by reordering his basic phrases and subtly changing his strumming patterns (compare the different four-line "stanzas" on CD track 12).

CD track 12, Raul Quispe, tuta kashua *(trans. L. C. Ballón/ T. Turino)*

00:02 Fade in, instrumental *charango*

00:09 Phrase 1 (h), *Chola munasqaytas* (The girl that I want)
00:11 Phrase 2 (l), *Wikch'usaq nishani* (I am thinking about abandoning her)
00:13 Phrase 1 (h), *Chola munasqaytan* (To the girl that I love)
00:15 Phrase 2 (l), *Saqisaq nishani* (I am thinking about leaving her)
00:16 Stuttering cadence

00:18 Phrase 1 (h), instrumental *charango*
00:20 Phrase 2 (l)
00:22 Phrase 1 (h)
00:24 Phrase 2 (l)

00:26 Phrase 1 (h) *Chola qawasqaytas* (The girl I am looking at)
00:28 Phrase 2 (l) *Saquisaq nishani* (I think I will leave her)
00:30 Phrase 1 (h) *Chola munasqaytas* (The girl that I love)
00:32 Phrase 2 (l) *Wikch'usaq nishani* (I think I'll leave her)

00:34 Phrase 1 (h), instrumental *charango*
00:36 Phrase 2 (l)
00:38 Phrase 2 (l)*, note varied order of phrases
00:40 Phrase 1 (h)*

00:42 Phrase 2 (l)*
00:44 Phrase 2 (l)*
00:46 Phrase 2 (l)*
00:48 Phrase 1 (h)*

00:51 Phrase 2 (l)* *Espejoy ventana* (Window of crystal)
00:53 Phrase 2 (l)* *Riskupin kashanki* (You are in danger)

00:55   Phrase 2 (l)* *Sh'allurunaymanta* (Of breaking)
00:56   Phrase 1 (h)* *P'akirunaymanta* (into small pieces)

ACTIVITY 2.2 *Paying close attention to the end of phrases and the strumming patterns, finish the chart noting melodic phrases (h versus l), vocal and instrumental sections, and where variations of any type occur.*

After learning to play the *tuta kashua*, the next stage of courting involves the boy hovering around the girl of his dreams in the market, strumming this tune. Sometimes this is just a general show of interest, but approaching festivals will also inspire boys to redouble their efforts to hook up, as we saw with our friend in Langui. As a part of festivals in district capital towns, young Caneños come together to dance the *punchay kashua*, or day dance (CD track 10). This often takes place slightly outside the main arena of festival activities, e.g., on a side street leading into the plaza. The *kashua* dance is done in a circle with the girls on one side and the boys, playing their *charangos* together in unison, on the other. Just as different wind instruments are not mixed in Conimeño ensembles, here only *charangos* are played together. The mixing of different instrumental timbres for contrast is a hallmark of the cosmopolitan 'folkloric' style (see Chapter 5), but it is typically not an indigenous practice.

In addition to rotating the circle with a simple shuffle step, the boys and girls sing in a shouting style back and forth to each other almost as if in a song duel. There are lots of different verses for this song; some illustrate the playful nature of courting:

Boys:	*Let's go, let's go*
	On this road above
	Let's go, let's go
	To the place of the party [night dance]
Girls:	*I cannot go*
	On this road above
	I cannot go
	To the place of the party
Boys:	*A devil like you*
	Makes one jealous
	A devil like you
	Makes one jealous.

Girls:	You cannot seduce me
	To go
	I am not easily fooled
	To go there.
Boys:	Behind your house there are three bad eggs
	Behind your house there are three bad eggs
	Your three friends are against me
	Three competitors are against me.
Girls:	Who doesn't know
	That you are filthy like a pig?
	Who doesn't know
	That you are filthy like a pig?

Those Canas girls are hard-core; this is tough love.

In Conima, men and women typically socialize separately at public events but do dance together as couples, sometimes holding hands. In Canas, the *kashua* dance circle and the singing are divided by gender. There are implicit couples in public *kashua* dancing, but the boys and girls stand across from each other on the male and female sides of the circle. Once a boy and girl have come to an understanding—initiated by wooing in the market and made public among their peers in the *punchay kashua*— they may take part in the *tuta kashua*. This is a private party among teens held in the hills outside of villages and towns. I was told that a boy will stand some distance from his beloved's house and play the *tuta kashua* tune on his *charango*, calling her out. They then join their friends at the agreed-upon spot to dance and sing to the *tuta kashua* music all night. It is said that at such occasions couples may make love for the first time, having agreed to marry. Thus, the words of the *tuta kashua*—let's go, let's go, to the place of the party—have a special meaning. In the days after the party, the couple may tell their families of their desire to wed and ask permission, leading to formal conversations between the parents. If all is agreed upon, they then enter a period of trial marriage, living together but without a formal ceremony, which comes later.

The *tuta kashua* tune is strongly associated with this final phase of the courting process. Thus, when a boy plays this tune to a girl in the plaza, he is telling her of his desires and intentions. Like the *charango* itself, the tune is a potent associative sign that communicates all this directly and safely, initially without the awkwardness of words. Musical meaning and communication—whether it is to express a particular social identity or, in this case, to express a particular desire and emotion—often occur through the repeated associations of instruments and sounds with particular things that the sounds come to stand for (just as the "Wedding March" can come to stand for weddings and marriage in our society). Such associative *signs* (also called *indexical signs*) have a special potential to condense a great deal of meaning. In a sense, the *tuta kashua* tune encapsulates the entire courting process, and all the emotions and desires involved through its most potent association with the culminating event of the *tuta kashua* party and what everyone knows can go on there. When the boys sing "Let's go, let's go to the place of the party," the words express only partial truths; the tune expresses more truthfully and more directly what they really mean.

ACTIVITY 2.3   *List all the ways you can think of that music is used for "courting" in your own society. Do some of these instances have features in common with the use of* charango *music in* Canas?

In Canas, I observed two other uses of the *charango*. Boys play it by themselves for entertainment and perhaps to practice, while alone pasturing their family's animals, or while walking to their agricultural work (Figure 2.6). Males of any age might also play *papa tarpuy* music for dancing and singing during breaks in communal agricultural work, the tune and context signaling another meaning for *charango* performance beyond its strict courting connotations (CD track 13).

Elsewhere in the Andes, the *charango* may have a variety of local contextual associations within indigenous communities. In certain provinces of Huancavelica, Ayacucho, Apurimac, Cusco, and Puno in Peru (see Figure 1.3), the instrument is associated with courting as it is in Canas. In northern Potosí, Bolivia, a strongly indigenous region, the *charango* is used for a dance that precedes ritual battles between communities from different districts (ritual battles are also a tradition in Canas). Tom Solomon reports for the same region that the small, round-backed *charango* was historically associated with dry-season festivals and especially Easter, whereas a larger, flat-backed indigenous guitar variant known as *qhunquta* was played at rainy-season festivals, especially Carnival; as in Conima, seasonal associations with particular instruments are common in indigenous Andean communities. During the 1960s and 1970s, a medium-sized, flat-backed *charango* became popular in northern Potosí and led to the decline of strict seasonal and contextual associations for the two original stringed instruments, indicating ongoing processes of change.

FIGURE 2.6 *A young man walks to work in the fields playing his* charango *in Canas. He has his digging stick, an agricultural tool of pre-Columbian origin, tied on his back.*

Beyond these more specific associations, Solomon notes that among indigenous Quechua speakers of Potosí, stringed instruments are played mainly by young unmarried men and are intimately associated with courtship. Exactly paralleling the situation in Canas, Solomon writes

> Once a man marries, he must put away his *qhunquta* and *charango*, and if an older married man were to pick up a stringed instrument

and play it, it would seem an absurd sight, even laughable, since it would look like the man was trying to "pick up" a younger girl. On the other hand, when some people commented negatively on how a man of about 45 who had been a widower for three years had recently been seen practicing on a *qhunquta,* others defended him saying that since he was no longer married and lacked a companion, it was his right to play and thus indicate that he was thinking of remarrying and had begun looking for a partner. (1997:118)

Beyond the local differences and striking similarities of meaning that the *charango* can convey across regions, an underlying indigenous musical trait is the close association of given instruments, genres, and dances with particular times of year, festivals, and social functions. Thus, although using the European model of the guitar, indigenous *charangos* are fashioned, tuned, played, and contextually associated in a manner that is specifically guided by general indigenous Andean approaches and values. It is through this process of incorporating a new innovation into an existing framework of cultural habits of thought and practice that the instrument became indigenous. Thus, indigenous Andean musical practices and styles do not have to remain static or be traceable to the pre-Columbian period to be considered "authentically Andean." The very introduction of strings into indigenous communities was itself a colonial innovation; the decline of seasonal associations with the different stringed instruments in Potosí after the 1960s is but one example of a more recent, locally generated change. Innovation, creativity, and change are constants in human societies. The important question for understanding cultural distinctiveness and identity concerns whose values and general tendencies guide the directions and meaning of practices and change. This issue will come into sharper relief through a discussion of the contrasting *mestizo charango* tradition.

THE *MESTIZO CHARANGO*

My fascination with the *charango* did not begin by working with indigenous musicians; it began during my first visit to the home of Julio Benavente Díaz in San Sebastian, a small town on the outskirts of Cusco city (Figure 2.7). After hearing a recording of an 'Andean folkloric group' at home, in 1977 I traveled to Cusco with the intention of studying the *kena* (end-notched flute). I asked around for a teacher, and a number of people pointed me to Julio Benavente. I arrived at his large, stately home; and after some initial pleasantries, Julio searched

FIGURE 2.7   *Julio Benavente Díaz, 1985.*

around for a *kena* and, finally locating one, played it for me. He was out of practice and could hardly blow it. He was terrible! Disappointed and somewhat troubled by the fact that he had come so widely recommended (was this the best Cusco had to offer?), I was about to politely take my leave when he pulled out his *charango* and said "I also play this." "Oh great," I thought, unimpressed by his previous attempt and his small instrument that reminded me of a ukulele. He had scarcely begun to play and I was totally hooked. The sound was huge and delicate and intricate; it was magical (CD track 14). We scheduled a series of lessons beginning that week, and I began my close friendship with Julio and his family that continues still.

Born in 1913, the son of a medium-sized *hacienda* (farm/ranch) owner, Julio grew up in the rural district of Huaracondo outside of Cusco city. Like other boys of this land-owning class, he came into close contact with the indigenous people who lived on and worked his father's land in what amounted to a sharecropper or peonage-type relationship. Beginning in the colonial period, Spaniards, *criollos*, and ultimately *mestizos* took or came to own large tracts of the best agricultural land in the highlands. Indigenous people entered into dependent relations with the landowners. In more remote or unattractive areas such as Conima and Canas, fewer *haciendas* were established, so there was more room for indigenous communities to maintain an independent existence.

Julio was born into a society founded on social inequality. Landowners depended on indigenous labor as the basis of their wealth, and as is typical of such situations, ideologies about the inferiority of the serving class were internalized by members of higher classes to rationalize the harsh inequalities. In the Andes, such ideologies included stereotypes of indigenous people as lazy, drunken, passive, backward, and stupid. As is also typically the case in such situations, prejudices against a given group of people are extended to their lifeways and artistic practices. Music and other expressive practices often become associative signs (or *indices*) that stand for the social group that produces them. If a social group is regarded as inferior, so will their art forms. To admit that an "inferior group" can produce superior music is to admit that its members might not be so backward after all, and this would raise doubts in relation to ideologies that rationalize economic inequality.

Nonetheless, the young children of rural landowners were surrounded by indigenous people. While Spanish was the prestige language spoken with parents in the home, they also learned Quechua. While raised Catholic, they also learned about indigenous spiritual beliefs and practices. Julio and others of his generation recounted how they grew up with indigenous music all around them, and some, like Julio, were fascinated and even learned to play instruments such as the *kena* and the *charango*. Parents might patiently disregard these activities among children, but Julio and others told me that as they approached young adulthood they met with fierce resistance from their parents, who regarded involvement with indigenous music as improper and an embarrassment. This, of course, was part of the unconscious process by which parents in many places instill social prejudices in their children. This is not done to be unkind; in early twentieth-century Peru, such attitudes were simply part of the social reality that the parents had internalized as children.

The young men of Julio's generation were certainly expected to leave their involvement with indigenous music behind when they were sent to Cusco or some other city for education; cities were the bastion of *criollo* and higher-class lifeways. But by the time Julio reached Cusco city for secondary education in the 1920s, something very significant was changing. Unlike earlier decades, he discovered that there were pockets of artists and intellectuals who not only did not distain indigenous music and cultural practices but actually celebrated them! He discovered that within such groups who met in coffee houses and *chicharias* (places serving indigenous corn beer and food) his knowledge of the *kena, charango,* and Quechua songs actually brought him popularity and prestige. He was hooked and continued to play and develop his abilities, especially on the *charango.* He was not alone. Others of Julio's generation, who self-identified as *mestizo,* told me similar stories. So what had changed?

With roots in the late nineteenth century, a variety of nationalist and regionalist movements known collectively as *indigenismo* (Indianist movement) emerged during the 1920s. Resulting from the independence wars with Spain in the 1820s, many of the original 'nations' of Latin America were defined as comprising relatively elite *criollo* and *mestizo* property owners. Indigenous people and those of African descent were excluded from the nation since they did not have full rights as citizens, as was true initially in the United States. Nations are identity units based on subjective feelings of belonging in relation to a given state. Social groups excluded from full citizenship typically do not feel part of the nation.

By the 1920s new, more inclusive conceptions of national belonging had begun to emerge throughout the Americas. This was partly due to changes in cosmopolitan nationalist ideology after World War I. Political legitimacy came to be grounded on the idea that each social–cultural unit—each 'nation'—should rule itself, i.e., have its own state or government, giving rise to the idea of the "nation-state." The expansion of capitalism in Latin America also favored more inclusive, populist conceptions of the "nation." Crucial for political independence, if Latin American countries were to gain economic independence, especially from the United States and England, they would need more 'national' consumers to support budding 'national' industries. Some Latin American leaders actually made it known that they regarded the consumption of 'national' products a patriotic duty. Thus, economic, cultural, and educational reforms were put in place to bring formerly marginalized groups into the countries' culture and economy. It was also necessary for the emerging Latin American capitalists to challenge the feudal power of the old landed elites, whose wealth depended on keeping the peasantry dependent and poor.

In places like Peru, where the indigenous peasantry represented a major portion of the population, freeing them from the old patronage system, teaching them "modern" (capitalist-cosmopolitan) lifeways, and linking them to the centralized state came to be seen as crucial for "progress." In a nutshell, economic progress and national sovereignty depended on converting subsistence farmers into modern wage-earning workers and consumers. All this began haltingly in Peru during the presidency of A. B. Leguía (1919–1930) and was continued to differing degrees by subsequent governments, especially the land reform that broke up the large *haciendas* under President J. Velasco (1968–1975).

Indigenous Andeans were useful to nationalist movements in other ways. If Peru was to assert its own distinctive cultural essence and quality as a nation, emblems from indigenous Andean, or "Inca," society provided the most vital signs of uniqueness. Thus, whereas indigenous music and dance had been disparaged by people of the upper classes previously, by the 1920s indigenous arts were beginning to be seen as valuable national or regional assets and heritage in *indigenista* circles. This was the situation when Julio and his generation arrived in Cusco and other Peruvian cities as young men. *Indigenismo* set the stage for the development of a unique *mestizo* style of *charango* performance—rooted in the regional indigenous styles of their rural homes but further developed according to *mestizo* aesthetics for presentational performance contexts.

The *mestizo charango* style was developed in Peru by Poncho Gomez Negrón, Julio Benavente, and Andrés Alencastre in Cusco; Felix Paniagua in Puno; and Luis Camasca and Jaime Guardia in Ayacucho among others (Figures 2.8–2.10). These prominent men adopted the strumming styles and some of the repertory from indigenous players from their rural home regions. Thus, within the *mestizo* tradition, there were regional substyles. But instead of just strumming their instruments as peasant *charanguistas* do, *mestizo* performers added a new plucked style of performance, which Julio referred to as *t'ipi* (Quechua: "pinch") using the right thumb and index fingers. Julio and other *mestizo* players alternate strummed sections with plucked sections in which they play the melody and a second harmony line together in a series of two-finger diads—largely in parallel thirds with occasional fifths, octaves, and unisons (CD tracks 14–16).

Mestizo players emphasized that the plucking technique was important because it allowed them to render the melody clearly and distinctly, whereas in the strictly strummed style, the melodies got lost in the dense, buzzy texture of open-sounding strings. The practice of plucking a melody with a second parallel thirds harmonic line was

FIGURE 2.8 *Poncho Gomez Negrón*, mestizo indigenista *musician from the province of Chumbibilcas, southern Cusco. Here, he is dressed as a* Qorilaso *horseman from his home province.* (Photo by the famous Cusqueño photographer Martin Chambi, used with the kind permission of his daughter Julia Chambi. Date of the photo uncertain but probably taken in the 1930s.)

already a common one in the *criollo* guitar style in Peru (e.g., for playing waltzes), and in fact, the use of parallel thirds is a common *mestizo* musical trait in Latin America from New Mexico to Chile. In a typical performance, *mestizo charanguistas* alternated strummed chordal sections at cadences, plucked melodic sections, and sometimes

FIGURE 2.9 *Andrés Alencastre,* hacienda *owner in Canas and known throughout Peru as an* indigenista *poet who wrote in Quechua. Photographed by Martin Chambi as a young man; here, Alencastre is dressed in the festive clothing of the indigenous people of his Canas region. The photo was taken in the fortress of Saqsahuaman above the city of Cusco, most likely in the late 1930s. (Used with the kind permission of Martin Chambi's daughter, Julia Chambi.)*

strummed melodic sections (à la indigenous practice), which they explained was important to create contrast and interest in the music (CD tracks 14 and 17). A rapid alternation of strumming and plucking is heard on "Cuando te conocí," a piece of the *wayno* genre in ABB form by Julio Benavente (begins at 3:08 on CD track 16).

FIGURE 2.10   *Augusto Chacón and family,* vecinos *of Tinta, Province of Canchis in southern Cusco, dressed in festive indigenous clothing of Canchis.   (Photo by Martin Chambi, used with the kind permission of Julia Chambi.)*

This desire to create contrasts and interest in the music was linked to another innovation within the *mestizo charango* tradition. In indigenous events, the *charango* was used to accompany participatory singing and dancing; thus, the dense, optimally loud and rhythmic strumming style served such purposes well. In the context of the *indigenista* movement, however, *mestizo* players began to perform on stages for urban audiences

"Cuando te conocí," performed by J. Benavente

3:08 Strummed introduction V-i chords
3:12 A section, phrase *a*, plucked melody
3:14 Strummed cadence
3:15 Phrase *b*, plucked melody
3:17 Strummed cadence
3:18 B section, phrases *c* and *d*, plucked melody
3:23 Strummed cadence
3:24 B section, phrases *c* and *d*, plucked melody
3:30 Strummed V-i chords
           (Song repeats a second time)

ACTIVITY 2.4 *Compare Benavente's style (CD tracks 14–16), with Valdez's style (CD tracks 17 and 18) and the indigenous charango players on tracks 12 and 13; in a few sentences, describe the differences as well as similarities in the sound. Pay special attention to variations in the density/clarity of the sound.*

in Lima, Cusco, Puno, Arequipa, and other cities. For example, the government of President Leguía sponsored staged "folkloric" festivals and performance contests in Lima to demonstrate the rich "national" heritage of Peru (see Chapter 4). Here, the concepts of "folkloric" and "folklore" refer to the idealized and stylized presentation of the arts of one social group (in this case, indigenous people) by and/or for another group (*mestizos* and *criollos*), often for nationalist and other ideological or commercial purposes. In Cusco city, an urban-*mestizo* performing troupe known as Centro Qosqo de Arte Nativo was created to perform representations of indigenous music and dance on stage for Peruvian urban audiences and, by the 1970s, tourists; Julio performed with this group for years, as did some of his children. In this context, music that had originally been played for participatory events was transformed so that it might be attractive in presentational performances for silent, seated, nonparticipating audiences.

The requirements for successful participatory and presentational performance are very different and sometimes diametrically opposed. As we have seen in both Conima and Canas, long repetitive performances that eschew dramatic contrasts and that emphasize loud volume and dense textures are fundamental to inspiring nonspecialist participation and helping community members get, and stay, in sync with each other. The pleasure is in the doing—dancing, singing, blowing, strumming—and the emotional power of such performances ultimately derives from feeling directly and intimately connected to the other participants. The very same sound features that make participatory music work, however, lead to boredom and inattention in presentational settings for a nonparticipating audience. In presentational performance, continual contrasts and sonic changes (which usually have to be planned and rehearsed in advance to go smoothly) are crucial for maintaining the attention and interest of the audience. Likewise, textural and melodic clarity are important so that an audience can discern and follow what is happening musically. The same is true for the visuals of dance.

'Folk' dances must be varied and made more dramatic if they are to entertain a nondancing audience. In the folkloric *indigenista* stage presentations of an indigenous courting dance using the *charango*, for example, a skit was created and standardized. As I witnessed in various folkloric presentations, at the end of the performance the women comically lead their "subdued" men away bound with ropes. Although perhaps done for entertainment value, the image produced is one of emasculated indigenous men. Political issues of one social group (*mestizos*) controlling the public images of another less powerful group (indigenous peasants) enter in here. Although *mestizo indigenista* performers intended to celebrate and 'preserve' indigenous traditions, the requirements of presentational performance in combination with their own internalized stereotypes of indigenous people often influenced the form and meaning of their performances.

In addition to such folkloric presentations, Julio Benavente and other skilled *charango* players began to perform live solo concerts on radio and on theater stages. In this type of setting, they began to create contrast in other ways. Whereas indigenous *charanguistas* will play the same tune or genre throughout a given event, as we have seen, *mestizos* wanted to 'elevate' *charango* performance by demonstrating that any musical genre could be performed on the instrument. *Mestizo* musicians might play an indigenous tune to demonstrate the roots of the instrument, but they quickly moved to performing a variety of genres, variety itself being an important value in presentational settings.

At the center of the *mestizo charango* repertory is a song–dance genre known as *wayno* (or *huayno*, pronounced "wino"). The *wayno* is a couples social dance. The songs are strophic, often with four-line stanzas (and no refrains or choruses) and short musical sections often in AABB form (a common form for European and North and South American social dance musics), ABB (as for "Cuando te Conocí," CD track 16), ABA, AABBCC, or other variants. The sections comprise two or more short phrases. After Benavente's lengthy introduction, "Sonquito Corazoncito" (CD track 14) is in AABBCC form and illustrates the common indigenous Andean trait of intensive repetition of melodic material across sections. In fact, after the introduction, the entire song involves a repetition and reordering of four short phrases. This *wayno* is from the Department of Puno and is actually structured like the indigenous wind music of Conima in terms of form and phrase repetition. *Mestizo indigenista* performers typically adapted indigenous pieces in this way.

Soquito Corazoncito, wayno, *J. Benavente*, **charango**, *and R. Bohorquez, guitar*

Time	Section
00:04	Introduction
00:28	Strummed V-i cadence
00:31	A section, phrase *a*
00:34	Phrase *b*
00:37	Phrase *c*
00:40	A section, phrase *a*
00:43	Phrase *b*
00:46	Phrase *c*
00:49	B section, phrase *b*
00:52	Phrase *b*
00:56	Phrase *b*
00:58	Phrase *c*
1:02	B section, phrase *b*
1:04	Phrase *b*
1:08	Phrase *b*
1:11	Phrase *c*

1:14 C section, phrase *d*
1:17 Phrase *d*
1:20 Phrase *a*
1:22 Phrase *b*
1:25 Phrase *c*
1:29 C section, phrase *d*
1:31 Phrase *d*
1:34 Phrase *a*
1:37 Phrase *b*
1:39 Phrase *c*
1:43 (Intro and piece repeats)

As its most important defining trait, the *wayno* rhythm subtly moves between an eighth-and-two-sixteenth-note rhythm and an eighth-note-triplet feel within simple duple meter; frequently, a three-beat measure will occur at cadences. For people who do not grow up with *wayno* music, this rhythm is difficult to master or even hear. I had been studying and playing *charango* with Julio for some months and thought that I was playing the *wayno* correctly. One day we were playing with some of his older friends in a *chicharía*, and at one point they turned to each other and said, with real pleasure, "He [meaning me] has finally got it." Got what? I thought. It turned out that I had been playing the rhythm wrong for months without even knowing it but unconsciously, through imitation, finally internalized the correct rhythmic feel, again without knowing it. Such subtleties often make all the difference, marking musical insiders and outsiders.

ACTIVITY 2.5 *Listen to CD track 15, Benavente's* wayno *"La Mala Yerba," several times and tap your finger with the guitar's bass pattern to get a feel for the* wayno *rhythm and its variations.*

Waynos have a bimodal quality, with phrases often alternating between the relative major and minor (e.g., A minor and C) but cadencing finally in the minor. This minor quality sometimes leads cosmopolitan listeners to associate the *wayno*, and Andean music more generally, with sad or somber emotions. Actually, the minor key has no such associations for either indigenous Andeans or *mestizos*. Among all the *mestizo* musical genres, *wayno* lyrics cover the broadest range of topics. Julio was a prolific composer of a variety of genres, but he told me that if he really had something important or heartfelt to express, he would compose a *wayno*. He composed *waynos* on joking themes, about love, expressing political protest, about places he has lived, and about the beauty of his surroundings using the same minor mode for all. One of his most famous compositions known throughout Peru, "La Mala Yerba," refers to the "bad grass" that grows in cemeteries covering the dead and is a song addressing issues of mortality and death (CD track 15).

In addition to the *wayno*, Julio and others of his generation also commonly performed *yaravís*, slow lyrical songs on sad romantic themes with the music alternating between or simultaneously juxtaposing 3/4 and 6/8 meters. Known as *sesquialtera*, this type of rhythm is common in *mestizo* music throughout the Americas, including the Mexican son discussed by Daniel Sheehy in his book on *mariachi* music in this series. Julio played this genre in a particularly free way with a meterless quality at cadences (CD track 16, hear also track 22). *Mestizo* players also commonly perform *marineras* on the *charango*. This song–dance genre is in faster *sesquialtera* rhythm and emphasizes the major mode; the entire form is repeated twice—the *primera* and *segunda* sections of the dance (CD track 17). In concert presentational performances, Julio would alternate genres with different meters, tempos, and rhythms to keep the music varied and interesting for audiences. Julio developed the practice of coupling contrasting genres such as a *yaraví* with its *"fuga de wayno"* (CD track 16) or *marineras* with *waynos* in medley for dramatic effect.

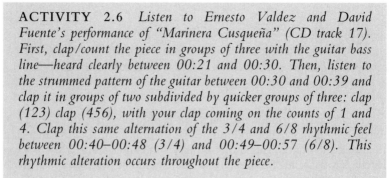

ACTIVITY 2.6 *Listen to Ernesto Valdez and David Fuente's performance of "Marinera Cusqueña" (CD track 17). First, clap/count the piece in groups of three with the guitar bass line—heard clearly between 00:21 and 00:30. Then, listen to the strummed pattern of the guitar between 00:30 and 00:39 and clap it in groups of two subdivided by quicker groups of three: clap (123) clap (456), with your clap coming on the counts of 1 and 4. Clap this same alternation of the 3/4 and 6/8 rhythmic feel between 00:40–00:48 (3/4) and 00:49–00:57 (6/8). This rhythmic alteration occurs throughout the piece.*

FIGURE 2.11 *Julio Benavente, portrait by Julia Chambi, contracted by the author for the jacket of an LP recorded by the author and released by UNESCO, 1982.*

Between 1977 when I met him and the early 1990s when he died, Julio performed concerts throughout Peru, in the United States, England, and other parts of Europe; he also recorded several albums (Figure 2.11). By this time he had retired from his lifelong career as a schoolteacher and educational administrator and could devote himself more fully to his music. He also continued to perform on radio, with friends at informal get-togethers, and especially for family celebrations in his home. Julio and his wife Alicia have eleven children and over thirty grandchildren.

Every birthday and every other family celebration was held in the patri-archal home. After the large meal served on such occasions, Julio would take out his *charango* and play *waynos*, *marineras*, and the occasional waltz for everyone to dance, accompanied on guitar by his son-in-law Raul Bohorquez or by me on *charango* or other friends who might be available. None of his children or grandchildren learned to play; but they loved to dance, and they loved his music. In these participatory family fiestas, Julio might occasionally play a melody in plucked style, but for the most part he would strum the melody as forcefully as he could, much like an indigenous player might, to keep everyone dancing.

At such times, the distinctions between the indigenous and *mestizo* styles melted away. Julio was adept at both participatory and presenta-tional performance and would alter his playing to fit the situation. This example suggests that many of the distinctive features of the *mestizo charango* style were developed to suit presentational performance. But *mestizos'* innovations and their very emphasis on presentational perfor-mance also index broader differences between indigenous and *mestizo* musical/social values—especially *mestizo* musicians' modernist concerns with musical development, improvement, and artistry for its own sake, as well as the status granted to cosmopolitan contexts such as concerts.

INDIGENOUS AND *MESTIZO* STYLES COMPARED

Differences between the indigenous and *mestizo charango* styles might be summarized by the following chart.

Indigenous Style	Mestizo Style
Smaller instruments	Larger/deeper bodied instruments
Numerous thin metal strings	Different gages of metal or nylon strings
No central bass string	Central bass string
Largely strumming	Strumming and plucking alternated
Strummed melody with open drones	Plucked melody, European harmonies
One or two genres tied to contexts/use	Wide variety of genres
Participatory performance	Participatory and presentational performance

Indigenous players favor smaller instruments strung with ten to fifteen thin metal strings. Melodies are strummed within the multiple open (drone), buzzy strings, creating dense textures and stronger rhythm. The instrument is used as a melody instrument (like indigenous winds), and there is little or no conceptualization of harmony. Tunings are regionally varied and sometimes even vary with the repertoire for a given context (e.g., in Potosí, Bolivia); the specifics of musical style typically identify specific community and regional indigenous groups. High-pitched tunings are favored, in keeping with indigenous predilections for high-pitched sound; *charangos* should "cry out like a cat." The instrument and specific tunes and genres are strongly linked to, and identified by, specific uses, occasions, and occasionally times of year, as is the case for most indigenous instruments.

Mestizo charanguistas favor greater musical clarity and contrast. Although some musicians of Julio's generation played metal-stringed instruments, they added thicker-gage strings to produce lower pitches more clearly and a low octave E string in the middle course to augment bass on the instrument. By now, most *mestizo* players prefer larger, round- or flat-backed instruments with nylon strings, which produce a clearer sound (nylon strings resonate less than metal strings). The plucking style added melodic clarity, and the alternation of strummed and plucked sections added contrast. *Mestizo* players approach the instrument with a combined melodic and harmonic conception. The typical Latin American *mestizo* musical trait of parallel thirds is used in melodic sections; by now, *mestizo* players strum full triadic chords, including V7-i at cadences, based on European harmony. *Mestizo* players pride themselves on being able to play a wide variety of general musical genres that are not tied to specific contexts or functions, and they will alternate different genres for contrast in presentational as well as participatory occasions. Wanting to show that the *charango* could play any genre, some *mestizo* musicians took particular pride in playing the *vals criollo* (*criollo* waltzes). Beginning as a working-class popular music in Lima, the *vals criollo* has by now become strongly associated with Limeño society more generally, and it carries a particular prestige because of this association (CD track 18).

The performance of indigenous and local *mestizo* music in concerts, contests, and other types of presentational situations was a new innovation that emerged within the early twentieth-century cosmopolitan discourse of populist nationalism. This same process of adopting and adapting local Andean musics to cosmopolitan cultural aesthetics and contexts continues in the early twenty-first century; many of the features that distinguish the *mestizo charango* style from indigenous *charango* performance also define the cosmopolitan 'folkloric Andean style' that has spread to the folk festivals and subways of the world (see Chapter 5). In the following chapter, however, I turn to another type of *mestizo* musical tradition and occasion—dance dramas performed in local patron saint festivals.

CHAPTER 3

Dance Dramas in *Mestizo* Catholic Festivals

∞

Every year, soon after mid-day on July 15, the *Chuncho* king and his warriors mount horses and gallop through the main streets of Paucartambo, a sleepy town on the eastern slopes of the Andes in the Department of Cusco, Peru (see Figure 1.3). Arriving at the church, they dismount and ascend the steps, standing at disciplined attention in two lines before the main entrance. Their musicians, who ran behind the riders, playing all the while, now stand to one side—two players of wooden transverse flutes and two drummers with bass and snare. As the musicians play on (CD track 19), the *Chuncho* warriors dance across the open space from one line to the other, spears held in front, heads and tall feathered headdresses held high (Figure 3.1). A crowd of spectators begins to gather. The music stops and the king leads his men inside to the altar, where they kneel and pray to the *Virgen del Carmen*, the patron saint of Paucartambo and subject of veneration during these, her *fiesta* days. The flute music of the *Chunchos* and the sounds of horses echoing off the newly whitewashed adobe—sounds heard at this time, on this day, for as long as people can remember—communicate that this year's *fiesta* has begun.

After emerging from the church, the *Chunchos* dance again while another band, with *kenas*, violin, accordion, harp, and drum, can be heard approaching (CD track 20). The head of the *Qolla* dance troupe leads a 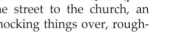 llama laden with animal pelts, clay pots, sacks filled with herbs, and other goods for trade. Accompanied by their band, the *Qolla* (pronounced "Koya") dancers move down the street to the church, an unruly lot, walking in and out of stores, knocking things over, roughhousing with each other and people they meet (Figure 3.2). They too dance on the church steps and then enter to pay respects to the Virgin by singing her a special song. If the *Chunchos* have pride of place by initiating the *entrada* (opening of the festival) on horseback and being

FIGURE 3.1 Chuncho *dancers on the church steps during the* entrada *of the Fiesta of the Virgin of Carmen, Paucartambo, Cusco, Peru.*

the first to dance, the *Qollas'* special status is marked by being second to perform and being only one of two groups who sing to the Virgin at the altar.

The *Qollas* are followed by dance group after costumed dance group, each with their own band: the *Qhapaq Negros* (rich and powerful negroes), the *AquaChilenos* (enemy Chileans), *Los Doctores* (officials and lawyers), the *Majeños* (liquor traders from Arequipa), and the *Saqras* (devils), among others. Each takes a turn dancing before the entrance of the church and then moves to the altar to pray. Unlike the other groups, however, the *Saqras* do not enter the church, for it would not do to have devils in the Virgin's sacred presence (Figure 3.3).

While the members of all these costumed dance groups are *mestizos* from the town of Paucartambo, throughout the *fiesta* days for the Virgin of Carmen (July 15–18), they stay in character and live the characters that they are presenting through dance. Local merchants, shopkeepers, teachers, farmers, students, and workers as well as Paucartambinos who have moved elsewhere but have returned home to perform become

FIGURE 3.2 Qolla *dancers approaching the church during the* entrada *of the Fiesta of the Virgin of Carmen, Paucartambo, Cusco, Peru.*

devils, lawyers, enemy Chilean soldiers, drunken liquor traders, African slaves, noble jungle Indians, and *Qolla* traders from the *altiplano* region of Puno. The men who dance as devils personally might wish to enter the church and pray to their patron saint, but staying in character in the *fiesta* performance takes precedence and precludes it.

There are many ways to tell the story of a given town and to express what is important about being from there. Paucartambinos do it through costumed dance dramas and music during their patron saint festival. This chapter explores two primary themes of this book: the ways music and dance communicate and realize social identities and how history is embodied and communicated through performance. The deep meanings and old histories expressed through music and dance in Paucartambo can be gleaned from the structure and performance of the festival as a whole, through learning the stories behind each individual dance group, and by understanding the social dynamics and status hierarchy that shape group membership and the prestige of a particular dance troupe. Certain dance troupes—especially the *Chunchos*, the *Qollas*, and the *Saqras*—are crucial to the main narratives of the festival,

FIGURE 3.3 Saqra *(devil) dancers in procession, Fiesta of the Virgin of Carmen, Paucartambo, Cusco, Peru.*

and they play prominent roles regardless of the social status of their members. Other dance troupes—especially the *Qhapaq Negros* and the *Majeños*—have risen to prominence within the *fiesta* structure because troupe members are wealthy or influential people in town who can hire the best bands, buy the best costumes, and throw the best private parties—thereby attracting other members of choice. Much can be learned about the town by studying both the narrative importance and the social importance of particular troupes.

I am using the term *dance drama* to refer to costumed/masked festival dances that enact or allude to particular characters and narratives. Dance dramas are a pan-Latin American tradition from New Mexico to Chile and are enacted in indigenous as well as *mestizo* communities. The roots of Latin American dance dramas are to be found in pre-Hispanic masked dances in the Americas, in European carnival traditions, and in religious plays that were used to attract and convert indigenous peoples to Christianity during the colonial period. Many of the dances done in Paucartambo are also performed elsewhere in the Department of Cusco for other festivals. Some of the characters, such as devils, jungle Indians, and people of African descent, are presented in dance dramas in other parts of the Andes and in Latin America more broadly. According to Henry Stobart, the two most famous dance dramas in Bolivia are the *diablada* (devil dance) and the *morenada* (black slave dance) (1998:292). Originally associated with Carnival in Oruru, these dances, accompanied by brass bands and with highly ornate masks and costumes, are now popularly performed in other parts of Bolivia as well as in Puno, Peru. In Oruru, the devils were associated with the underground in relation to the dangerous work in the mines, a major occupation there. Thus, the meanings behind a given dance drama, even ones that are widely diffused, often pertain to local situations.

Community identity stands at the center of the meanings conveyed by dance dramas in many parts of Latin America. This is often accomplished negatively, i.e., by portraying outsiders as threatening, as uncivilized, or in a satiric manner. In Paucartambo, the *Saqras* represent the ultimate outsiders threatening the mundane world. The *Qollas* (*altiplano* traders), *Majeños, AquaChilenos* (Chilean invaders during the War of the Pacific, 1879–84), *Doctores, Chukchus* (malaria victims from the jungle), and *Qhapaq Negros* all represent different types of outsiders. In the 1981 Paucartambo *fiesta*, a small ad hoc group of young men dressed up as hippie tourists with backpacks, floppy hats, and toy cameras, which they shoved in people's faces while asking stupid questions in bad Spanish. Although not having all the trappings of an official dance group (band, sponsors, participation in the festival's main events, longevity), the "hippie tourists" illustrate how the newest wave of foreign intrusion became the object of creative parody; this group also suggests how new dance troupes might have been created in response to particular historical experiences. Insider social identities are always partially produced by defining who and what "we" are not; in Paucartambo, an array of foreigners are depicted through dance, often in rather unflattering terms. For historical reasons, discussed below, the *Chunchos* (jungle Indians) represent the inhabitants of Paucartambo. As such, they are given pride of place in a number of festival events, and their demeanor throughout the festival days is dignified and proud, providing a positive self-portrait of Paucartambinos.

The Festival of the Virgin of Carmen in Paucartambo is a particularly interesting case through which to study dance dramas because of the local specificity of the various stories being told and the richness of the narratives. Peruvian scholar Gisela Cánepa-Koch notes that many of the dances done in Paucartambo originated there but have been diffused to other towns in Cusco. She writes that Paucartambo "is regarded [as] an important center for the creation and propagation of dances from the Department of Cusco, due to the number of dances performed there, the dancers' innovations, and their successful participation in contests and regional folkloric events" (1995:3).

Historically, there was a custom in Paucartambo that each man should dance all the different roles over a lifetime; but in actuality, the dance troupes have become like social clubs, and many people join together with friends and family or people of similar social status to dance in the same troupes year after year. In the period leading up to the festival, troupe members come together to rehearse and socialize. Until recent decades, female dramatic roles in groups like the *Saqras*, *Qollas*, and *AquaChilenos* were danced by men; but now women are taking these roles. The *Qollacha* dance is one of the few that prominently includes women. In this dance, young *mestizas*, wearing white lacy blouses and velvet skirts, basically represent themselves; young men and women may pair off, or it may simply be danced by women.

The dance troupes have a hierarchical structure, with a leader who organizes rehearsals and directs the choreography. During the main events of the festival, the dance troupes are involved with presentational performance. That is, they present pre-rehearsed choreography for a variety of different figures, with set music, for an audience of onlookers who do not participate in the performance. At certain times during the evenings, however, the performances shift from presentation to participatory dancing. In the streets and plaza of the town, the troupes' bands begin to play popular *waynos* and *marineras* (see Chapter 2), and spectators may join in dancing with the bands of their choice.

Unlike the dancers, the bands accompanying the troupes are hired professionals or semiprofessionals from elsewhere. The hired ensembles have to learn the music that is used for a given dance year after year and that, like the costumes, is a stock part of the drama presented. The music used to accompany most dance troupes during their performances is based on well-known Peruvian *mestizo* genres, including the *pasacalle* (procession music), *waynos, marineras*, and hymns. The first three are usually in short sectional forms such as AABB (CD tracks 20–23).

ACTIVITY 3.1 *The form of the different pieces can be charted in seconds using the counter on your CD player. For example, the* Majeños *theme (track 21) would be charted as follows: 00:00—section B, 00:05—section B, 00:10—section*

A, 00:15—section A, 00:20—section B, 00:25—section B.
Using the seconds counter on your CD player, make a time chart
indicating each A and B section of the vocal part for CD track 23
(e.g., 00:16—A, 24—A, 00:32—B, 00:37—B).

Three types of musical ensembles perform in Paucartambo: side-
blown flute and drum bands (CD track 19, Figure 3.4); *orquestas* typically
comprising two *kenas*, one or two violins, harp, accordion, drums, and
sometimes mandolin (CD tracks 20 and 23; Figures 3.5, 3.6); and brass
bands (CD tracks 21, 22; Figure 3.7). The *orquestas* illustrate an interesting historical layering of musical influences from a variety of local and
foreign sources. They combine *kenas*, a flute of Andean pre-Columbian
origin, with harp and violin, European instruments that were initially
adopted by indigenous and *mestizo* musicians through the influence of
colonial missionaries in the sixteenth and seventeenth centuries. Marching
band-style drums were diffused in Peru during the republican era of the

FIGURE 3.4   *Flute and drum band accompanying the* Chunchos, *Fiesta of the*
Virgin of Carmen, Paucartambo, Cusco, Peru.

FIGURE 3.5 Orquesta *of Cusco accompanying the* Qollas, *two* kenas, *harp (played upside down), two violins, accordion, drums, mandolin.*

nineteenth century. The accordion was invented in Germany in the 1820s but did not become popular in Peru until the first half of the twentieth century. The densely blended tone colors of the *kenas*, violins, and accordion create a sound unique to these ensembles. These instruments play the melody, while the harp (played upside down when walking) provides the bass line and the drum accents the melody and dance movements or plays the rhythmic underpinning for a given genre.

ACTIVITY 3.2 *Compare the sounds of the* orquestas *accompanying the* Qollas *and the* Qhapaq Negros *on CD tracks 20 and 23, respectively, as they alternate with the dancers' singing. The sounds of the violins, kenas, and accordion playing the* Qollas' *music are well blended. Listen closely and try to identify the sounds of the flutes (kenas), the violins, and the accordion playing the melody in unison. If you listen closely to track 20 at 1:20–1:25, you can also identify the mandolin. Notice how*

FIGURE 3.6 Orquesta *of Cusco accompanying the* Qollas, *two* kenas, *harp (played upside down), two violins, accordion, drums, mandolin.*

the different melody instruments subtly come in and out of the foreground. On track 23, the Negros' orquesta *has the same instrumentation but the accordion is more prominent; notice that around 1:25 and 2:06 the* kenas *come into the foreground more clearly.*

Certain dance troupes always use the same type of musical ensemble, and its sound is an important index of their characterization. Other troupes may hire whatever type of band they can afford. Loud volume is a particular asset for attracting spectators to a particular dance troupe both during their presentational performances and during the periods of participatory dancing in the streets. Brass bands are the most expensive to hire and, because of their cost and volume, are the most prestigious type. Second in size, volume, and expense are the *orquestas,* and finally the flute–drum bands—usually two wooden transverse flute players, snare drummer, and bass drummer—are the

FIGURE 3.7   *Brass band of the* Majeños, *Fiesta of the Virgin of Carmen, Pau-cartambo, Cusco, Peru.*

cheapest and least prestigious. It is odd then that the *Chunchos*, the most important group to the narrative of the *fiesta*, always perform with a flute–drum ensemble. In this case, the instruments and music played are intended to sound like the music of Amazonian tribes; that is, the music, like the costumes, is a key part of the dramatic represen- tation. By custom, rather than any dramatic significance, the *Qollas*, *Saqras*, *Chilenos*, *Negros*, and many others are accompanied by *orques- tas*, the most common type of band (CD track 21). The *Majeños*, on the other hand, hire a brass band because of the wealth of troupe members and as a sign of that wealth. Affluence and power have become a key part of the character presented by the *Majeños* as well as being based in actuality; thus, their use of a brass band both has dramatic signifi- cance and is made possible by the social status of the membership. The case of the *Waka Waka* (mock bullfighting) troupe illustrates fluidity in the types of bands hired due to economic considerations. In 1977 the troupe hired a single flute player and one drummer because they had fallen on hard times and this was all they could afford. By 1981, however, the troupe had been reorganized with better sponsorship from more wealthy new members and consequently hired a small brass band.

THE VIRGIN OF CARMEN

Each Andean town large enough to have its own church has a patron saint who is considered the special protector of the people who live there. Many towns celebrate their patron saint's feast days, assigned by the Catholic calendar, with customs similar to the event being described here, although Paucartambo is particularly famous for its numerous dances and the elaborateness of its festival.

The Virgin of Carmen, embodied by a statue housed in the church, stands at the center of the celebration. In Paucartambo, the statue of the Virgin is considered by some almost as an animate being. Just before the festival, the statue is dressed in new garments and made ready. Some Paucartambinos say that the facial expression of the Virgin (statue) changes; if she looks happy, they will have a good year; if she looks pale or sad, trouble lies ahead. Furthermore, people also say that that the Virgin's mood, and thus the future, is affected by the quality of the *fiesta* held in her honor.

Statements about religious beliefs are often difficult to interpret. Some people seem to literally believe that the quality of festival performance actually affects the Virgin's shifting moods, which in turn directly affect the town's well-being. These beliefs, however, can also be interpreted metaphorically. In fact, there is a clear correlation between the quality of the *fiesta* and prosperity in the town. For instance, during bad economic periods, it is simply harder to put on a lavish event; and during good times, people will have more resources and spirit for the celebration. The level of investment, spirit, and participation that goes into the festival thus actually serves as a direct index of the well-being of the town and a portent of the near future. Given that this correlation is repeatedly experienced, it may be that people simply interpret "the mood of the Virgin" as a direct sign of "the mood of the people." Beyond this, Paucartambo's festival involves a series of activities that bond the people to the place and to each other—this in itself is a source of well-being.

At least during my period of research in the late 1970s and early 1980s, some older people in Paucartambo connected the idea of the Virgin as source of well-being to the concept of *Pachamama* (Earth, living force of the Earth, Earth mother; see Chapter 1). The practice of associating male Catholic saints with indigenous mountain divinities and the

Virgin with *Pachamama* has been widely reported in the Andean region. This type of religious *syncretism* (blending of concepts from different spiritual orientations) is but one example of the processes of cultural syncretism that in fact define *mestizo* lifeways.

FESTIVAL ACTIVITIES

Many of the focal events of the *fiesta* are centered around the Virgin, but a variety of things go on and are accomplished during the celebration. The major sponsors of the festival and of individual dance groups fulfill their social responsibilities to the town, their friends, and their neighbors and gain prestige and influence as a consequence. Participation in a given dance group helps fortify friendship and family relations. The general revelry that takes place in the streets throughout the *fiesta* bonds the community as a whole and certainly has a cathartic function for individuals.

As described for the opening of the *fiesta*, each dance group, excepting the *Saqras*, enter the church to pay homage. After all the dance troupes have danced on the church steps and paid homage to the Virgin of Carmen during the *entrada*, they disperse to different parts of town. Some groups parade to the central plaza one block away, where they continue their presentational performances for the amusement of the onlookers. Others return to the private homes of their group's sponsor or leader to eat and drink and party among themselves. This type of ad hoc activity goes on throughout the night—parading and performing in the streets, partying at someone's home. Around 8:00 on the evening of July 15, the dance ensembles and their bands return to the central plaza to perform. Here, they dance simultaneously in different parts of the plaza and in neighboring streets. After a while, they cease to do their specific dances and their bands might begin to perform well-known *waynos* and *marineras* for general dancing. At this point, the presentational aspect of the dance groups' performances breaks down and the festival becomes a huge participatory event, with people dancing to the band of their choice. At around 10:30, a huge display of fireworks is set off. A standard feature of patronal *fiestas*, the size and splendor of the fireworks display is one criterion by which the success of the festival, and the generosity of the main sponsor, is judged.

There is a *serenata* (serenade) for the Virgin at midnight on July 15, ushering in the central day of the *fiesta*. As a show of stamina and devotion to their saint, troupes return to do their presentational dances on the church steps in turn. Because of fatigue and excessive drinking, some troupes do not show at the *serenata*, but key groups such as the *Chunchos* and the *Qollas* would be widely criticized if they did not take part.

On the morning of July 16 in 1977, a high wooden platform laden with lowland agricultural goods (nuts, fruits, coca, sweets, and coffee) was erected in the town plaza. Several men threw the food to the crowd gathered below (in 1981 the platform was not used and these goods were thrown from a balcony in the plaza). While Catholic beliefs and practices predominate in Paucartambo's *mestizo* festival, this event harkened to a pre-Columbian practice. The early Spanish chronicler Molina de Santiago reported that in 1535 Manco Inca held *Inti Raymi* (Festival of the Sun, June) festivities, which included an event where agricultural products were thrown to the common people. The Peruvian writer Luis Valcarcel describes a widespread harvest dance around a tree laden with fruits and gifts; at the end of the dance, the tree is shaken and its contents are consumed by participants. The distribution of agricultural foodstuffs in Paucartambo suggests the embedding of indigenous practices and ideas within this Catholic *mestizo* festival but in inverse proportion to indigenous festivals such as that for the *Virgen de la Candelaria* in Conima (see Chapter 1). In Conima, a Catholic name was used for what was really an indigenous agricultural festival; in Paucartambo, the distribution of food was only a vestige of indigenous harvest rituals in a primarily Catholic event. As this comparison shows, the distinction between Andean indigenous and *mestizo* lifeways is a matter of the degree of prominence of indigenous versus Iberian or cosmopolitan models for belief and practice.

Masses are held for the Virgin on July 16 and 17, and throughout the *fiesta* days there is a constant stream of people praying and paying homage in the church. On July 16 and 17, the statue of the Virgin is placed on a heavy litter and carried in procession throughout the town (Figure 3.8). These processions are headed by the priest, the *fiesta* sponsors, and town dignitaries accompanied by a brass band. Acting as honor guard, the *Chunchos* dance around the litter as she is carried through the streets, and the rest of the dance groups and bands follow behind. Processions of this kind are common to patron saint festivals throughout Latin America.

Various scholars have noted that the routes of processions often serve to define the geographical boundaries of a community. Thus, processions communicate community identity concretely in relation to geographical residence. Furthermore, carrying the sacred icon through the streets sanctifies what is usually a secular social space. In Paucartambo, the route of the Virgin's procession circumscribes the central plaza

FIGURE 3.8   *Procession of the Virgin of Carmen.*

(the core of the town) and then leads to the extremities of each street, stopping at the point where it leaves the town proper. Ultimately, the saint is carried past every house, and some people open the front windows looking out onto the street as well as the back windows of their homes. It is said that the Virgin's goodness enters through the front and drives evil out the back, blessing and purifying each home as she passes. Dramatizing this belief, during processions the devil dancers climb onto the rooftops along the route and, as the saint passes, shield

FIGURE 3.9 Saqra *dancers on the rooftops during the procession of the Virgin; the devil in the foreground shields his eyes as the saint passes.*

their eyes from her glory and then disappear to the back side of the roofs—concretizing and communicating through art what people think is happening in the houses below (Figure 3.9).

During the evening of July 16, dance troupes perform in the plaza and the streets and the presentational performances give way to general participatory dancing and revelry. July 17 begins with an early-morning mass, followed by the dance groups proceeding to the cemetery, where they dance and commemorate the graves of members, family, and friends who have died recently. This is followed by the second, shorter procession. At around 2:00 in the afternoon, people begin to congregate in the central plaza for the dramatic climax of the festival—a mock battle between the *Chunchos* and the *Qollas*. As 3:00 approaches, the *Maqtas* (costumed clown figures who serve as policemen during the festival) move the crowds back by spraying beer and cracking their whips. The battle arena takes the form of a circular track around the plaza. The *Qollas* and other dance groups enter, moving around the plaza. Finally, the music of the *Chunchos* can be heard approaching; and with their coming, the battle begins.

The mock fighting proper takes place between the *Chunchos* and the *Qollas*. Some members of other dance groups remain in the performance space and engage in horseplay to add to the general excitement. The *Saqras* (devils) pull a flaming wagon around the ring in which they "collect the souls of fallen combatants" and thus have a more formal dramatic role to play. The *Chunchos* and *Qollas* begin to attack each other with their spears and whips in the fashion of mock fighting and at times bring each other to the ground in an actual wrestling match. When a dancer is "killed," he will briefly stay down and then get up to fight on. After about thirty or forty minutes, as the battle moves to a close, *Qollas* who are killed stay down. Finally, the headman of the *Qollas* is killed, signaling their annual defeat. The *Chuncho* king captures the headman's wife (historically danced by a man), takes her for a turn around the plaza, and then leads her and his men away.

Dramatic battles of this sort are a part of many Andean *mestizo fiestas*; a good example of one in the northern Peruvian sierra can be seen in John Cohen's excellent movie *Mountain Music of Peru*. These mock fights are related to colonial conversion plays such as *The Battle of the Christians and Moors* but also to actual ritual battles that take place throughout the Andes, famous examples being in Canas, Cusco, and various parts of Bolivia.

Documented as a pre-Columbian Inca practice, ritual battles took place between the young men of the upper and lower moieties of Cusco. Contemporary ritual battles take place between different neighboring indigenous communities. In the one I witnessed in Canas, combatants fought with slings and rocks as well as with lug nuts tied to the end of whips. The goal of the fighting was to drive the opposing side to their end of the battle plain, thus controlling the field. On hills above the battlefield, women sang and danced the *kashua* of Chiaraje (name of the battle's location) and prepared food for the festive mid-day meal with their men. In these battles, one or more deaths may result and real wounds are common. Yet, participants commonly described the battles as "a beautiful game," and a few people told me that the blood that was shed served as a sacrifice to the Earth, benefiting all. As depicted in Paucartambo's mock fight, it was customary in the actual ritual battles of Canas for the winners to steal women from the opposing side and to take them home for a period of time. The mock fight between the *Chunchos* and the *Qollas*, however, communicates a particular set of meanings that are specific to Paucartambo. Before the battle between these two groups can be understood, it is necessary to explore the meanings of the groups themselves.

THE DANCE TROUPES

It is no accident that the *Chunchos* lead off the *fiesta* on horseback and with dancing for the *entrada*, serve as the honor guard and protectors of the Virgin during processions, and annually win the mock battle with the *Qollas*. In the context of Paucartambo's festival, the *Chunchos* are the heroes and the "home team." Located in a highland river valley, Paucartambo ("place of flowers") is on the eastern slopes of the Andes and was a doorway to the Amazonian lowlands. One local legend has it that *Chunchos* were the original inhabitants of the Paucartambo area. This idea makes sense from a historical perspective. During the Inca period, the empire was divided into four quarters, or *suyos*. Writing around the turn of the seventeenth century, the chronicler Guaman Poma de Ayala stated that Antisuyo extended east from Cusco into the Amazon jungle and, hence, included Paucartambo. Guaman Poma uses the terms *Antis* and *Chunchos* as synonyms for the people of this region and depicts a *Chuncho* representative of Antisuyo, complete with feathered headdress like the ones used by Paucartambo dancers, in a drawing of the Inca's royal council. Thus, the idea of "noble" *Chunchos* is an old one and is fitting for Paucartambo. It also makes sense historically that *Chunchos* have come to represent Paucartambo insiders in the drama of the festival, whereas in some Andean regions jungle Indians are portrayed through dance as uncivilized savages and outsiders. It is striking that such old histories and emblems (e.g., the feathered headdress) are kept alive and communicated through dance even after the basis of those histories is generally forgotten.

The *Chuncho* costume in Paucartambo maintains some of the features used to represent Amazonian Indians generally: the carrying of spears and especially the tall feathered headdress. The Paucartambo *Chunchos* wear masks made of screen painted red, with blue eyes; coins and bangles hang from the nose, depicting wealth. The *Chuncho* king wears a gold crown, a long blue cape, and a maroon vest and knee breeches with fringe sewn around the knees. Knee fringe was a sign of nobility among the Incas, and knee breeches and capes were worn by the Spanish colonial elite; hence, the costume fuses signs of elite status from both societies. The *Chuncho* soldiers wear short capes, white shirts, skirts of various colors, and a religious emblem depicting the Virgin on their chests. Some of the *Chunchos'* dance figures are based in the twin line formations of the European (French and English) contra dance. The movements and "body language" include a lunging step (described by people in Paucartambo as a "war-like leap") when crossing the lines and stiff standing at attention, expected of disciplined soldiers, while in line.

The *Chunchos'* music is considered to have a martial quality, in keeping with their character. The music used for the *entrada* and when they are on the move, for example, is in 2/4 march time, with rolling snare and bass drums heard prominently. It is also considered to resemble the music of jungle societies. The *Chunchos'* march opens with a single statement of an A section followed by a B section, which can be repeated anywhere from two to six times depending on the performers. The descending cadence formula is the same for the A and B sections; motivic repetition across sections is common in indigenous music generally (see Chapter 1).

ACTIVITY 3.3   *The form of the* Chuncho *march heard on track 19 is A (00:01), B (00:07), B (00:11), A (00:15), B (00:22), B (00:25). Using the seconds counter on your CD player, make a timeline chart for the rest of CD track 19 indicating the A and B sections. More detail could be added by charting the descending cadence phrase (**b**):*

Section:	A	B	B
Phrase:	*a* (00:1) *b* (00:05)	*c* (00:7) *b* (00:9)	*c* (00:11) *b* (00:13)

Paucartambinos' assertion that the *Chunchos* music resembles that of jungle Indians is supported by a recording made by Willard Rhodes (Folkways FE 4458) of the Cocama and Shipibo tribes of the upper Amazon. On this recording we hear flute, snare, and bass drum ensembles performing tunes with forms and undulating melodic shapes similar to the *Chunchos'* music. Similar to the feathered headdress, which has long been associated with jungle Indians, the *Chunchos'* music likewise becomes "part of their costume" through a sonic resemblance with the music of the actual people they are representing.

Throughout the festival days, the *Chuncho* dancers maintain a dignified and disciplined deportment, as befits soldiers and the honor guard of the Virgin. For example, the dancers should not drink much, be seen intoxicated, or act out in public in other ways; and they are expected to be prompt in their ceremonial duties. For this reason, dancing in this group might not be considered to be as fun as dancing with the *Qollas,* who are supposed to drink a lot and act outrageously, or the *Majeños,* who, in their role as drunken liquor traders, can actually get drunker than skunks themselves and rationalize that they are only staying in character. Thus, although the *Chunchos* are the most prestigious group in terms of the *fiesta* narrative structure, it is not one of the most popular groups to dance in; and during the years of my research, it actually had some trouble filling the ranks.

In contrast, the *Qollas* offer the best of both worlds. In terms of narrative importance, they are second only to the *Chunchos*; but because they represent "savage" *puna* (high regions above the tree line) dwellers and traders of the *altiplano* (high plateau) region of Puno and Bolivia (formerly Collasuyo, or *Qolla*suyo), they are supposed to act wild throughout the festival days. Such "poetic license" leads to a great deal of fun. In my experience, valley dwellers in the Peruvian highlands have a fear of, and prejudicial attitudes toward, *puna* dwellers. For instance, one time when I was setting out from the Vilcanota valley for the Canas region above (see Chapter 2), a woman begged me, with tears in her eyes, not to go there because those *puna* savages would surely murder me. Had she ever been in Canas, I asked. No, she replied, but she had heard what they were like. Such are the attitudes that lie beneath the depiction of the *Qollas* in addition to the simple fact that they are outsiders from another region. To depict their wildness, the *Qolla* dancers roughhouse in the streets and act in a surly manner. They carry whips and in one part of their dance, known as *Yawar unu* (blood water), take turns pairing off to raucously whip each other's ankles and calves in the center of the dance circle.

The people of the Peruvian and Bolivian *altiplano* region are also famous as long-distance traders and herbalists. In the dance troupe, the *Qolla* headman and his wife lead a llama carrying trade goods to represent this aspect of their character. Hand movements used when dancing and in procession depict them spinning wool as befits llama herders and wool traders. A main portion of their dance has them moving forward with quick steps, body turning side to side, as if they were in the act of traveling, spinning as they go. In a special market that takes place during the festival days in Paucartambo, actual traders from the *altiplano* region come to sell the same types of products featured in the *Qolla* dancers' dramatization. Here, art imitates life, and the longevity and importance of the *Qolla* dance communicate the historical longevity and importance of trade between the eastern slopes of the Andes and the *altiplano* region.

The *Qollas* are also depicted as having a poetic, sentimental side. This is expressed in their devotion to the Virgin and in the songs they sing for her during the *entrada* (CD track 20). In one of their songs, "Qolla

Kaspapa" (I am a *Qolla*), they identify themselves and express their sensitive nature:

> *Here Lady, we arrive from our town Paucar* Qolla.
> *Llama driver (I am),* Qolla *(I am).*
> *Our souls we are guiding,*
> *With our sins tied with ropes,*
> *Only you Lady untie.*
> *Five roses in your hand,*
> *You are God's Lady,*
> *Angels count.*

When this song is performed for the Virgin, the *Qollas* sing in unison with a relatively smooth, clear, but forceful vocal style. The song is performed in a serious, somber manner in moderate tempo as suits the occasion and to express their serious, romantic side. Acting as a kind of theme song for the group, it is also sometimes sung in procession and when dancing in the plaza. In contrast to the softer, romantic aspect of their character communicated through their wistful songs, other songs are faster and more raucous and the vocal timbre employed is coarser—closer to shouting—expressing their wild, savage side (CD track 24). Thus, through costumes, props (the llama), and especially dance movements, songs, and vocal style, the *Qolla* dancers bring a multidimensional character—rough and savage, wistful and romantic—to life.

The rough-edged part of the *Qolla* character is easily understood in relation to them being *puna* dwellers and outsiders to Paucartambo. The wistful, sad mood they create is related to feelings of loss and separation from the Virgin. This part of their characterization and the narrative importance of the *Chunchos* and the *Qollas* in the *fiesta* more generally can be understood in relation to various local stories told about their rivalry involving the Virgin.

In one story, the statue of the *Virgen del Carmen* originally belonged to the *Qollas* of Puno. One year when the *Qollas* were transporting the statue in procession, they were attacked by *Chuncho* warriors, who, victorious, took the statue of the Virgin and put her in a river, where she was found by Paucartambinos, who then housed the statue in their church. In another variant, after the *Chunchos* defeated the *Qollas* in battle, they carried the saint back to Paucartambo and placed her in the church for safety. In yet another story told to me, the Virgin originally belonged to Paucartambo. One time, *Qollas* came to town and attempted to steal the statue but were attacked by *Chuncho* warriors, who won the day and returned the Virgin to her church for safety.

Villasante Ortiz (1980:135–136), a scholar of Paucartambo, cites another story. In the sixteenth century, two statues of the *Virgen del Carmen* were sent over from Spain, one destined for Paucartambo and the other for Paucarqolla (Department of Puno). The statue brought to Paucartambo was much larger and more beautiful than the one received in Paucarqolla. Discovering the discrepancy, some Paucarqolleños traveled to Paucartambo with the claim that a mistake had been made. No change was instituted, however, and thus "*Qollas*" continued to return to Paucartambo each year to pay homage to "their" statue and to trade with the valley community.

The plot thickens, however, because in Ocongate (located some fifty miles south of Paucartambo) a similar mock battle between *Chuncho* and *Qolla* dancers takes place during the festival of Corpus Christi, and the Virgin of Carmen is not even involved. As reported by David Gow, in that town the *Chuncho–Qolla* rivalry is explained with another story. People fleeing a famine on the *altiplano* sometime in the past immigrated in large numbers into the Ocongate area, and a battle ensued as the original inhabitants tried to repel the *Qolla* invaders. As in Paucartambo, *Chuncho* dancers have come to represent the original inhabitants of Ocongate (also in the former Antisuyo region), but in that town the mock battle between the *Chunchos* and *Qollas* has a different meaning, involving economic competition over land rather than competition over the Virgin.

The point here is not to determine which stories are true but rather to suggest that many layers of history and local meaning are encapsulated and relived each year through festival performance. In many stories told in Paucartambo, the *Chunchos* are indirectly or directly responsible for the Virgin's presence in the town; and as the provider of all good things, the Virgin is central to Paucartambino identity and well-being. The *Chunchos'* role as honor guard during processions and their annual victory over the *Qollas* communicate all of this and more.

As we have seen, the *Saqras'* primary role is to serve as a foil to the blessed Virgin. The characters presented are Lucifer and his consort, the *China Saqra*; his court of eight or more male dancers; and a young boy and girl—"little devils." The male dancers wear plaster masks depicting hideous faces of animals and monsters, each sporting a pair of horns and carrying a cane. They wear blond or red wigs, multicolored striped tunics, and knee breeches with red stockings and knee fringe (worn by the Inca elite). The flared cuffs of their tunics, along with the knee breeches and stockings, again call to mind the dress of colonial Spaniards. The mask of the *China Saqra* depicts a smiling, particularly fair-skinned, woman with blue eyes (Figure 3.3). Like the aspects of *Saqra* costume, their dance seems to be a parody of elite Spaniards or *criollos*. In one figure, they dance in a circle, hooking their canes together in the center and promenading around the axis with the free hand placed on the outside hip in a mockingly genteel manner. In another major dance figure, they politely perform a Spanish quadrille—all of this creating a funny contrast with their grotesque faces and wild hair. Their true nature comes out in the finale of their circle dance, however, when they perform *zapateo* (fast foot-tapping dance) accompanied by a ruckus of grunts and animal noises. The *Saqras'* particular depiction of what evil looks like may be interpreted at a variety of different levels.

By the end of the 1970s, the *Qhapaq Negros* had recently been reconstituted as a major dance group. The addition of the term *Qhapaq* (rich and powerful) to their name is odd in that originally this dance depicted black slaves brought into the Andean region, similar to dances done elsewhere in the Andes. This troupe was reconstituted by a group of relatively well-to-do Paucartambinos who lived and worked in Cusco city. They were able to afford beautiful costumes and were the one group that actually changed costumes several times during the festival (altering the color but not the design) to increase their spectacle and garner prestige. Besides the *Qollas*, they were the only other group who had the honor of singing to the Virgin. Whereas the *Qollas'* songs functioned to express their special relations to the Virgin and to fill out their dramatic role, this honor was granted to the *Qhapaq Negros* because of the social prestige of troupe members. During the *entrada*, they carried several small altars lined with candles to the church as gifts for the saint and addressed her in song: "Refuge of the sinners, comfort of the afflicted, aid to the captives." Their splendid costumes, beautifully rehearsed line dances, sentimental song, and clear devotion to the Virgin all made them a favorite at the festival. The black ceramic masks with exaggerated "African" features are the last vestige of caricature common to other such dances in the Andes. Rather than being satirized as outsiders, the *Qhapaq Negros* create and are received as a sympathetic portrayal of human suffering and the Virgin's benevolence.

In contrast, the *Majeños'* dance is at least in part a satire of exploitative outsiders. By the nineteenth century, alcoholism had become a serious problem in rural communities, a problem compounded by the cost and government taxes levied on commercial alcohol. The *Majeños* dancers depict liquor traders and muleteers who came from the Maje

FIGURE 3.10   Majeños *dancers with their horses and mules carrying kegs of alcohol. The big-nosed figure* (bottom left)*: is a* maqta, *or clown, who serves the role of policeman during the fiesta days.*

valley of Arequipa (hence the name) to sell alcohol in the Paucartambo region and elsewhere in Cusco (Figure 3.10). Like the *Qolla* dancers' depiction of Puneño traders who still actually come to Paucartambo to sell their wares during the *fiesta*, earlier in the twentieth century Maje liquor traders were in town to distribute alcohol at the same time they were being depicted in the *Majeños'* dance. Some people in Paucartambo actually refer to the group as *los Borrachos* (the drunks), and this aspect of their character is brought out by *Majeños'* staggering dance: bottles of alcohol held high, they lurch forward and back in time with the staggering rhythm of their theme music (CD track 21). Negative feelings toward the Maje traders are also made patent by the grotesque, leering faces of the dancers' ceramic masks.

In her study of this dance, Zoila Mendoza Walker suggests that in the early decades of the twentieth century *haciendas* (large farms/ranches) in Cusco took over the production of alcohol and, moreover, that the *Majeños* dance actually came to be performed by rich and powerful *hacienda* owners from the Paucartambo region. This connection explains the signs of wealth and prestige that are also part of the *Majeños'* contemporary characterization. The dancers dress well, in expensive leather jackets, riding pants, high leather boots, and broad-brimmed hats, and ride fine horses (a sign of wealth). Several members of the troupe play the role of servants, who lead pack mules with metal drums of "alcohol" as props.

The *Majeños* dance ceased to be performed between the mid-1950s and the mid-1970s. During that period, Peruvian president Juan Velasco (1968–1975) initiated a land reform that broke up the large *haciendas*. Thus, major landowners left the rural region for Cusco and other Peruvian cities. Velasco was a populist nationalist who encouraged cultural programs, festivals, and institutions to champion popular arts—redefined by nationalist discourse as "folklore." Already known for the wealth of their dance traditions, Paucartambinos were inspired by the new governmental support. Dances that had ceased to be performed, like the *Negros* and *Majeños*, were reestablished; furthermore, costumes and choreography were newly stylized for presentational performances at government-sponsored folkloric events and, through such events, popularized and diffused more widely. When the *Majeños* dance was reinstated in Paucartambo after 1975, the actual Maje muleteers and *hacendados* (*hacienda* owners) who had been associated with the troupe were now history. The *Majeños*, however, were reestablished by local well-to-do businesspeople, transport company operators, teachers, and government employees who wished to take up the mantle of the old elite. According to Mendoza, these individuals were particularly interested in associating themselves with the images of wealth, power, and prestige formerly belonging to the *hacendados* and Arequipa traders. To be true to the original meaning of the dance, in the spirit of "folkloric" authenticity, however, the Paucartambo dancers maintained the *borracho* images in the dance and insisted on details such as having cane alcohol in their bottles (the type sold by Maje traders) rather than the beer used by *Majeño* troupes in other towns. Thus, the present-day *Majeño* characterization is a blend of the original narrative meaning of the dance and images of wealth derived from the status of earlier *hacendado* troupe members and their contemporary correlates.

One of my favorite dance troupes in Paucartambo is *Los Doctores*, who parody local government officials, especially the *alcalde* (mayor), and lawyers. Versions of this dance are done in many parts of the Andes, but the role seems to have particular significance in Paucartambo. Writing in the 1940s, Bernard Mishkin noted that in Paucartambo the *alcaldeship* had lost all dignity and importance; phrases such as "dog and an *alcalde"* were used to express particular disdain. At that time (1946), the mayor was seen as the dupe and long arm of the governor. Hence, more than merely being an outsider, the *alcalde* was a traitor and the instrument of outside political domination.

The *Doctores* dancers wear tall black top hats, black coats with tails, and black pants. The ceramic masks depict fair skin, a large nose, and a sneering mouth. Each dancer carries a heavy law book, which he pounds with his free hand to the rhythm of the music. In the dance, the *Doctores* strut about in a line to the rhythm of a *passacalle* (march-like piece). At any time while walking through the streets, they might pick out an unsuspecting bystander, usually someone in indigenous dress, and drag him into the middle of their circle. In a none-too-subtle display of what they think of the law, they begin to beat him with their law books while simultaneously screaming different accusations of wrongdoing. The prisoner is then obliged to kneel down and beg for mercy before being released, much to the delight of the spectators who were lucky enough not to get caught.

As these descriptions indicate, the characterization of each dance troupe derives from and combines a variety of different historical, mythic, and social meanings: associations with the characters being presented as well as with the social status and aspirations of the people who have presented them over time. In some cases, such as the *Qhapaq Negros* and the *Majeños*, the meanings associated with the historical characters have blended with the status of troupe members to shape their artistic presentations. What is striking in other cases, especially the *Chunchos*, is that historical associations dating back even to the pre-Columbian period are brought to life and communicated through dance drama each year in this *mestizo fiesta*.

Some of the characters are complexly multifaceted. The *Qollas*, for instance, present an unruly, brutish character who is also poetic and sentimental; the *Chunchos* are jungle Indians who are also noble warriors; the *Majeños* are prestigious, wealthy, leering drunkards; the *Saqras'* presentation combines images of animals, monsters, and genteel Europeans. A universal function of art is precisely to combine ideas and images—even abnormal or contradictory ones—in new ways to make the complexities of experience and imagined possibilities patent in perceivable forms. The complexities of representation through dance dramas in Paucartambo make sense of the complexities of history, of individual personalities, and of abstract concepts such as "good" and "evil." During the *fiesta* days, Paucartambinos mingle on the streets and dance in the plaza with the personifications of evil, with Maje liquor traders/*hacendados*/economic leaders of the town, with Puno traders who in actuality are down the street selling their wares in the market, and with noble *Chunchos*, the "original inhabitants" of their region. They also rub shoulders with "rich" African slaves, enemy Chilean soldiers, and malaria victims; and they express to government officials what they think of them. Lining up in procession behind the Virgin, characters of history, of legend, of uncertainty, and of fundamental beliefs dance their stories so that the people of Paucartambo remember them and, thus, remember who they are.

ACTIVITY 3.4   *Make a list of the traditions in your own community that, like the* fiesta *in Paucartambo, function to tell and retell the important stories of your society (e.g., Thanksgiving plays in primary schools in the United States).*

Andean Music in Andean Cities:
The Case of Lima, Peru

Similar to the situation in the United States, many countries in Latin America underwent radical transformations beginning in the early twentieth century as people left their rural–agricultural ways of life and moved to cities in search of wage-based employment and better health and educational possibilities for their children. In the United States, there were massive migrations from the rural south to cities like Chicago and Detroit, and by the 1950s, new music scenes developed such as Chicago blues with the influx of people born in the Mississippi Delta—Muddy Waters, Howlin' Wolf, Elmore James, John Lee Hooker, Bo Diddley—and the possibilities for recording there provided by companies like Chess Records.

The commercial country music market also mushroomed in the United States as new urban industrial wage earners from the rural south and midwest had more income to spend on music, especially music that soothed nostalgic longing for their original homes and families' lifeways. In a very real sense, country music, and the radio programs, clubs, and dances where it was performed, provided much needed comfort for recently urbanized people to feel less alien, "to be themselves," and to socialize with other "hillbillies" who found themselves in Pittsburgh or Detroit. Parallel to the life experiences of the migrants, country music gradually changed to reflect a weakening of regionalism and integration into the U.S. mainstream; the highly polished production of a homogenous style of contemporary Nashville country music, heard from coast to coast, is the result.

Likewise, the populations of Latin American cities, especially the capitals, began to swell during the first half of the twentieth century. Whereas these cities were originally centers of elite *criollo* cosmopolitan cultural production and musical styles—symphony orchestras, operas, ballroom dance bands—by the 1950s, the soundscapes of Latin

American cities began to include regional rural-based styles from all over the given country. The fact that these transformations were happening in so many countries at relatively the same time suggests broader structural underpinnings.

Population growth, expansion of capitalist economics, and political nationalism worked together to fuel rural to urban migration. The original form of nationalism that shaped countries throughout the Americas in the late 1700s and early 1800s emphasized the participation of white male landowners and excluded women, indigenous peoples, and peoples of African descent from the voting citizenry. After World War I, the idea that unified cultural groups—"nations"—should rule themselves through their own governments in their own territories (their own states) became the predominant form of nationalist discourse underpinning political legitimacy throughout the world. Since countries like Peru and Bolivia had never been defined by a "unified cultural group," these states gradually began to develop economic, cultural, and educational programs to integrate the indigenous majority into the "national" mainstream. The presidencies of Augusto B. Leguía (1919–1930) and Juan A. Velasco (1968–1975) represent two major cultural nationalist periods in Peru.

At different historical moments, programs of national integration were explicitly designed to support capitalist development within a given country. It was correctly reasoned that Latin American countries could not be politically sovereign unless they were economically independent of powers like the United States and England, whose governments and corporations intervened in the policies of Latin American states for economic benefit. Economic independence depended on the development of local capitalist industries that were in turn dependent on a local workforce and, more importantly, a local consumer base—to buy the products the new local factories manufactured.

To this end, in the Andean countries it was necessary to transform indigenous subsistence farmers into "modernized" cash-earning peasants and members of the industrial working class. As indicated by his own statements, the educational, cultural, and land reforms of Peruvian President Juan Velasco were explicitly designed to create cash-earning workers and consumers. In addition to the state-directed educational and ideological pressures for rural people to modernize (a euphemism for adopting capitalist ethics and worldview), by the mid-twentieth century, population growth created land shortages that forced members of rural families into the cash-based economies; cities offered the greatest opportunities for jobs.

The capital city of Lima, Peru, and its port Callao had 645,172 inhabitants in 1940; by 1984 the population had grown to nearly six million. Rural to urban migration, with the majority of the migrants coming from the Andean highlands, accounts for much of this growth. Unlike Ecuador and Bolivia, where the capital cities are located in the highlands, Lima, Peru's most politically and economically important city, is located on the coast. In Peru, there was a major social, cultural, and economic divide between the coast and the highlands. The coast, and especially Lima, was the center of *criollo* society, and from a coastal perspective, the highlands were associated with Indians (Quechua and Aymara communities). Historically, there was social prejudice against indigenous peoples and highlanders in Lima and the music and lifeways that were associated with them. In the 1970s, anthropologist Richard Schaedel observed the following:

> Attributes of indigenous origin were simply not tolerated in Lima (e.g., Indian dress, barefootedness, coca chewing, Quechua speech). . . . It was clear that migrants who came to Lima were obliged to adopt *criollo* ways and suppress their ethnicity, and part of the *criollo* way was to accept their role as manual workers and subordinate people. (1974:402)

As Schaedel suggests, during the first half of the twentieth century rural migrants in Lima attempted to distance themselves from the cultural markers of their highland origins. Indigenous music was simply not a common part of the Lima soundscape beyond the confines of certain nationalistic, "folkloric" events and performances that emphasized idealized "Inca" (Cusco) imagery rather than the sights and sounds of contemporary highlanders from different parts of the country. This began to change in the 1950s, however, as more and more people from the different highland departments began to settle in Lima. This chapter chronicles the rise of highland Andean music in Lima as a resource for creating migrant social networks in the city and, as a prominent theme of the book, a means of communicating social identities. It will also be shown that the predominant ways people identify themselves and link themselves to others have a major impact on grassroots as well as commercial musical trends. In Peru, regionalism, rather than nationalism, remained the predominant anchor of social identity throughout the twentieth century.

NATIONALISM IN THE 1920s

Around 1900, Peruvian composer José María Valle Riestra produced *Ollanta*, an opera based on an Inca theme. Operas depicting exotic imagery including ancient civilizations and mythology were a common part of the opera tradition in Europe, and nineteenth-century operas, such as those of Verdi, were sometimes linked to nationalism. Valle's choice of an Inca topic fit both these cosmopolitan molds; images of Inca civilization were soon to play a key role in the nationalist discourse of President Leguía and Peruvian intellectuals of the 1920s.

In 1921, President Leguía proclaimed June 24 *Dia del Indio* (Day of the Indian) as a gesture to create links with Peru's indigenous population. In 1927, Leguía and the mayor of the Rimac district of Lima sponsored a "folklore" contest during the *Fiesta de San Juan* (June 24) for "vernacular [read highland] artists." Previously, the Fiesta of San Juan in Rimac had mainly featured *criollo* music. The 1927 event represents the first major public display of highland music in the capital, and an estimated 50,000 people attended the festival. The winners of the "folklore" music contest were a trio from Cusco who performed a *yaraví, waynos,* and "war dances" with two *kenas* accompanied by piano. Since piano is not typically used by indigenous and rural *mestizo* musicians, the presence of this instrument suggests that the performers were of Cusco's urban elite. The prize was awarded by Leguía himself. Commenting on a repeat of this festival contest in 1928, Leguía is quoted as saying

> Nothing better reflects the collective psychology as the music of the people. . . . In *our* Inca music exists the race and imperial power, the tragedy of the [Spanish] conquest . . . and the richness of an overflowing glory after this unfortunate event. . . . The vernacular artists that have come from all corners of the country to take part in this event attest to the marvels of *our* folklore. (quoted in Vivanco 1973:37 from the Lima newspaper *La Cronica,* 6/25/28, emphasis added)

Leguía's lauding of "Inca folklore" and "artists from all corners of the country" grew out of a concern to link the semiautonomous regions of the country to the central government, thus undermining the control of local landowning elites within a program of economic unification and "modernization."

Events like the San Juan "folklore" contest are a common device in nationalist movements. They are designed in a specific way to create an image of the nation and cement it in the minds of the populace. Unlike smaller social groups such as the family or local communities where people can identify with each other through face-to-face interaction, nations are particularly abstract identity groupings; most people will only know a fraction of the people and places that comprise the nation. So how is the idea of "nation" represented and communicated? Performing arts like music and dance often play a key role.

ACTIVITY 4.1 *Do a Web search on the annual Smithsonian Folklife Festival held in Washington D.C. What kinds of activities, arts, and artists are programmed? How is the festival described? Write a short essay about how this festival might contribute to conceptions of a national culture in the United States.*

"Folklore" festivals and contests are used in a similar way in countries throughout the world. In the San Juan contest in Lima, regional representatives were displayed together within the same event, thus creating a concrete portrait of the "nation" as the combination of all regions represented. Moreover, music provides attractive, emotion-laden signs of identity that make people feel proud and positive about the identity group being depicted. Notice that in Leguía's speech he said *"our* Inca music" and *"our* folklore." Formerly, the governmental elite in Lima would have ignored or even disparaged musical signs of highland identity such as the *wayno*; here, however, the president is claiming that the music represents not only its region of origin but Peru as a whole. The use of the word "our" in nationalist discourse creates the inclusive, collective idea of "nation," and in Leguía's speech helped guide how the collection of regional representatives on stage should be interpreted. The abstract idea of national identity is brought into being, communicated, and invested with emotion through the combination of such linguistic signs with the concrete, emotion-laden imagery provided by artistic performance. To be effective, such combinations have to be repeated again and again to make the new connections—between representatives of different regions or social groups and the ideas *'our* folklore' and *'our* nation'—appear commonsensical. The San Juan 'folkloric' event in Rimac and similar events elsewhere were repeated many times through the following decades.

Harking back to a country's glorious past is a standard feature of nationalist imagery because it inspires pride and suggests longevity. Whereas the Lima elite typically emphasized their European roots, in the context of 1920s *indigenista* nationalism, Leguía and other elite intellectuals began to symbolically identify with Inca high culture because this provided distinctiveness for the Peruvian nation in contrast to other countries.

ACTIVITY 4.2 *Investigate Inca society in a general reference source and then select a facet of Inca civilization that is of particular interest and prepare a five-minute report about it for your classmates.*

The emphasis on the Inca past and Cusco city, the Inca capital, also made it possible for the elite to avoid facing their own paradoxically prejudicial attitudes regarding the contemporary indigenous peasantry. Likewise, many of the *indigenista* (Indianist) musicians involved in presenting "Inca folklore" in the San Juan festival and other urban stage events during the 1920s were usually not indigenous themselves but rather of the higher social classes. For example, performers in the 1928 contest for "unpublished Inca music" included the best-known *indigenista*–academic composers of the highland urban elite, such as Teodoro Valcarcel from Puno and Policarpo Caballero from Cusco. *Estudiantinas* (large string/wind orchestras) including Centro Qosqo de Arte Nativo from Cusco, the group Julio Benavente played with (see Chapter 2), also performed in Rimac in 1928 (Figure 4.1). Clearly,

FIGURE 4.1 Indigenista *performance orchestra from the department of Ayacucho. Notice the performers holding the large scissors (*far right*) used as percussion instruments for the "scissors dance" (*Danza de las Tijeras, or Dasaq), one of the most famous traditions from Ayacucho. Also depicted are mandolins,* kenas, *harp, guitars, and* drums. *(Photo by Martin Chambi, used with the kind permission of his daughter, Julia Chambi.)*

this was not "Inca" or indigenous music but rather a folkoric rendition by middle-class *mestizo* performers. This situation soon began to change.

Peruvian musician and scholar Alejandro Vivanco observes that during the 1930s highland migrant performers gradually began to perform in the Rimac festival in greater numbers. By 1939 indigenous highland musicians also gained a presence, including Qhantati Ururi, an Aymara *sikuri* group from Conima whose trip to the capital was sponsored by *vecinos* from the town of Conima (see Chapter 1). More dramatically, by the 1950s, highland migrant musicians of the "popular" classes would begin to represent their own regions through music in the capital for themselves on records, on the radio, and in public performances every Sunday. The soundscape of the *criollo* capital began to change.

REGIONAL "COUNTRY MUSIC" IN LIMA

It takes a concerted educational effort over a long period of time to get people to strongly identify as a nation in relation to a preexisting state. It also takes more than symbolic gestures. Government leaders have to provide real benefits for the masses to win their loyalty and get them to identify with the nation-state. This did not begin to happen in relation to indigenous Peruvians until President Velasco's land-redistribution and rural school-building reforms beginning in the late 1960s. In addition, Velasco made Quechua an official language, instituted a media reform requiring more radio time for Peruvian music, and supported "folklore" festivals in an attempt to reach out to indigenous peoples. Nonetheless, national sentiment remained weak in Peru during the 1950s and 1960s, and highland migrants in Lima continued to identify most strongly with their local communities and regions of origin. It was these forms of identity that served as the basis for migrant musical activities, styles, and marketing through the 1980s. Replacing the elite-generated "Inca-Cusco" imagery of the 1920s, regional *wayno* music was fashioned to appeal to the huge new migrant consumer market. This music was performed by working-class highland migrants and heard in Lima on commercial recordings, in Sunday afternoon *coliseos* (tent shows), and on the radio.

Created by highland migrant musicians for highlanders in Lima, this new style of "urban-country music" paralleled the emergence of U.S. country music in the 1920s. It naturally grew out of, but was also consciously fashioned to index, regional highland *wayno* styles. Each area of the highlands has its own prominent ensemble types and distinctive dress. For example, the *orquesta* of Cusco, described in Chapter 3, consists of *kenas*, violins, harp, accordion, and sometimes drums. A major ensemble type for the Department of Ancash was a string band—guitars backing mandolin, violin, and sometimes accordion and *kenas* (CD track 25). The *orquesta* from the Department of Junin featured a harp and violin "rhythm section" accompanying a good number of saxophones and clarinets (CD track 26). Ayacucho was known for its guitar duos, guitar–*charango* trios, as well as harp accompaniment with intricate melodic runs inserted between the phrases of the main sung or instrumental melody (CD track 27). The distinctive sounds of these ensembles were strongly associated with their specific regions and could thus serve as signs communicating the identities of these regional groups. Junin, Ancash, and Ayacucho sent the first large waves of working-class migrants to the city; and artists from these departments became the first "country music" stars because they had the largest consumer bases to support them.

ACTIVITY 4.3 *In a few sentences, describe the different instrumental ensemble sounds of CD tracks 25, 26, and 27. Then describe the vocal styles on the three tracks in terms of the use of vibrato, vocal ornamentation, and pitch range. In your written description, underline what you find particularly distinctive about these examples compared to the music you usually listen to.*

In the highlands, these ensembles and the music they played would have been considered *mestizo*. In Lima of the 1950s and 1960s, however, the regional ensembles came to index "home" for migrants of both indigenous and *mestizo* backgrounds. Within regional migrant communities, the social distinction between indigenous people and *mestizos* continued to be recognized; from the Limeño perspective, all working-class highlanders were "Indians." The dynamics of self-representation were thus complicated. Some migrants attempted to avoid all external signs of their highland background in order to assimilate into Limeño society and, thus, publicly would not have been involved with highland music. Other migrants chose to unite with people from "home" as the best strategy for social survival in Lima. For the migrants who chose this path, the regional musical styles and the events where they were played were central to forging and sustaining communities. Within these regional communities, the indigenous–*mestizo* hierarchy would sometimes influence interactions; but when a united front was needed in relation to Limeños, other regional groups, or, for example, when seeking aid from the government, regional-community solidarity would be emphasized over the internal indigenous–*mestizo* divide. As discussed in Chapter 1, identities are always contextually relative according to specific needs, goals, and situations.

Describing the beginning of her professional career and the transition from idealized "Inca-Cusco" imagery to more realistic portrayals of regional identity, the famous Pastorita Huaracina (Maria Alvarado) from Ancash said that early on "I always appeared dressed as a Cusqueña [woman from Cusco] because I did not yet understand the difference, or how I could identify myself with my own region. I sang songs from Ancash but with Cusqueño dress." She went on to observe, "I made my debut months later with the name Pastorita Huaracina in Ancash clothing singing songs from Ancash although mixed with other songs from Huancayo or sometimes from Cusco" (quoted in Llórens, 1983:114–115). The choice of the stage name Pastorita Huaracina, "little shepard girl from Huaras," itself underlines nostalgic rural imagery as well as identification with a specific place in the Department of Ancash.

Whereas previously "Inca-Cusco" images were used to represent the whole of the sierra, as a critical mass of highlanders formed in Lima, they came to favor sights and sounds that reminded them of their specific homes. As in the case of Ms. Alvarado, migrant artists often took stage names that indexed their regional identity. But the performers and audience members were now also city dwellers and were aware of the "country bumpkin" stereotypes Limeños had regarding highlanders. As they gradually began to internalize urban-cosmopolitan aesthetics and attitudes, the migrant performers began to alter their style of presentation. Like country stars in the United States, female *wayno* singers wore fancy, stylized versions of regional-rural clothing. The multiple skirts and petticoats of female singers, typical of highland dress, were beautifully embroidered with idyllic rural scenes and imagery. Below the *cholita polleras* (skirts) they wore high-heeled shoes. The braids so often worn by *mestizas* in the sierra were replaced by permed hairstyles to communicate a new urban sophistication.

In terms of musical style, the high heels and perms were paralleled by the wide vocal vibrato which indexed cosmopolitanism while the upturned vocal ornaments and general timbre were part of highland style (CD tracks 25 and 26). In addition, the dense, undifferentiated textures of highland participatory performance began to give way to an emphasis placed on the individual soloist, usually the lead singer, and somewhat clearer or more separated instrumental parts. Open-ended participatory performance gave way to prearranged "closed" song forms common to cosmopolitan popular music, such as instrumental introduction, vocal verse, vocal verse, instrumental interlude, vocal verse, vocal verse, *fuga*. The *fuga* in commercial *wayno* music was an animated concluding section with new, shorter melody and text (1:41 in track 25). Thus, instrumental and vocal as well as sectional contrasts were emphasized whereas indigenous participatory performers tended to eschew contrasts of all types in their long, repetitive performances (see Chapters 1 and 2). All of these stylistic innovations are common to performers and genres that shift from participatory to presentational performance and to high-fidelity recording—i.e., from music meant for *doing* to music meant for *listening*. At a more specific level, however, the combined signs of regional highland identities and urban living both grew out of and communicated the life experiences of the migrants and so were authentic signs of their combined past-rural and present-urban experiences.

The development of the commercial *wayno* style parallels the rise of the *coliseos*, the main performance venue where this was presented live. Between 1938 and the early 1970s, more than thirty *coliseos* were created to host *espectaculos folkloricas* for migrant audiences. The *coliseos* were large outdoor spaces surrounded by a wall, either open or covered with a circus-like tent or tin roof. A stage was erected facing bleachers. Established as commercial enterprises by Lima entrepreneurs, highland musical performances took place mainly on Sunday afternoons and evenings, the only leisure time afforded most of the migrants who worked as maids, as laborers, and in factories. People from all over the highlands attended these events, and a parade of different performers took the stage in turn.

Each afternoon a few of the better-known artists, such as Pastorita Huaracina and Jilguero del Huascarán (Ancash); Flor Pucarina, Flor de Huancayo, and Picaflor de los Andes (Junin); and the male guitar–*charango*–vocal trios Lira Paucina, Trio Ayacucho, and Los Errantes from Ayacucho served as paid headliners to draw the crowds. The majority of performers were unknown and unpaid and took part either to gain exposure or simply for the joy of performing. Regional migrant clubs and ensembles from departments other than Ancash, Ayacucho, Junin, and Cusco also took part in relative frequency to the size of their migrant community (see map, Figure 1.3). For example, Puneño regional clubs performing *trajes de luzes* (costumed dance drama traditions) backed by brass bands occasionally performed in the *coliseos*, but working-class Puneño migration did not take off until the 1960s and so did not have a big impact on the migrant music scene in Lima until the 1970s. Outside the star category, many of the performers who took part in the *coliseos* simply presented their songs and dances as they would be done in the highlands—i.e., without the stylistic transformations discussed earlier.

The mainstay of the music performed was the *mestizo wayno*, along with other regional genres such as the *muliza* and *huaylas* as well as festival music and dances. The *wayno* stars sang newly composed songs as well as songs from home. Spanish, Quechua, or mixed texts on romantic-love themes were in the majority; but, like the performers' stage names, song lyrics often alluded to specific highland places and so became important "hooks" for the regionalistic audiences.

Gripping the microphone as a nightclub singer might, star performers would stand out in front of their bands on stage, making wide, expressive hand and arm gestures to connect with the audience. They sang in a heartfelt way combining wide vibrato, characteristic of urban music in Lima, with vocal ornamentation based in highland style (see Chapter 2). During instrumental interludes, female stars would hand the microphone to an attendant on stage and then dance a genteel *wayno* in high heels. Handclapping, verbal interjections, "down-home" jokes, shouts, and laughing during the instrumental interludes were used to create a fun, informal atmosphere and, in fact, to suggest the participatory social events where this type of music originally would have been played in the highlands. In the hostile environment of Lima, where highlanders were still considered aliens, these performances created a much needed space where the migrants were in the majority and could feel comfortable together. Through music, dance, and verbal performance, the *coliseo* acts also provided abundant reminders of the *fiestas* and other good times enjoyed "back home." It is no small wonder that the *coliseos* drew such large audiences and were so lucrative for their owners back in the heyday of the 1950s and 1960s.

Recording provided another outlet for commercial *wayno* music. RCA Victor published the first commercial recordings of highland music in 1928, the year after the San Juan "folklore" contest in Rimac was established. The first recordings were elite-stylized pieces like those performed in the contest in Rimac or cosmopolitan-influenced fusions like the "foxtrot *inkaico*" (Inca foxtrot) genre. Alejandro Vivanco suggests that 1947 marks the real beginning of the highland recording industry. In that year, the Peruvian novelist and anthropologist José María Arguedas, who was head of the "folklore" section of the Ministry of Education, convinced Odeon Records to publish several selections in the urban-country style by artists such as the Hermanitas Zevallos. Paralleling the phenomena of blues and "hillbilly" recording in the United States during the 1920s, the commercial success of Odeon's first sierra-music releases brought other companies to the field. Arguedas notes that by 1953 Odeon alone had expanded its "folklore" catalogue to include ninety-six records by Junin artists, nineteen from Ancash, sixteen from Huancavelica, fourteen from Cusco, and twelve from Ayacucho, again mirroring the size of migrant communities from those regions in Lima. By 1967, the number of commercial Andean records had surpassed three thousand, and by the 1970s highland music was outselling any other single type in the capital.

Supporting the record industry and *coliseo* performances, Andean music radio programs began in Lima with the show *El Sol en los Andes* (*The Sun in the Andes*) on Radio El Sol in 1951. Aired daily for an hour at six in the morning, this program featured live studio performances as well as recordings of *wayno* music. According to José Antonio Llórens, an expert on highland radio programming, in 1972 there were thirty-six such programs in the capital, nineteen of them on Radio Agricultura, a station created in 1962 to serve the highland population; in 1981 Llórens counted ninety-one different highland music programs in the capital (1985:12). Matching the growth of different regional migrant communities, as these programs developed they became more regionally specific. Using the names of the shows as indicators, Llórens found that in 1970 36% of the programs referred to Peru in general, 28% to the provinces in general, and 36% to the Andes in general with no specific regions being mentioned. In 1981, 20% of the shows retained the general Peru identification and only 14% referred to the Andes in general terms, whereas 52% were aimed at specific regional migrant communities. As might be guessed, the largest number of programs were aimed at the Junin migrant community (twenty-two programs); fourteen programs were directed at people from the Department of Ayacucho, eight for the Sierra de Lima, seven for Ancash, six for Cusco, three for Cajamaraca, one for Huanuco, and one for Puno (Llórens, 1985:12).

In hour or half-hour slots, these shows played music from the region in question, advertised upcoming musical and cultural events for that particular migrant community, and aired personal notices and greetings—e.g., birthday and anniversary salutations, messages for someone to get in touch with such and such a person, and family news. Since many migrants did not have telephones in the 1980s, these programs were a crucial source of information and communication for a regional migrant community spread over the expanse of the capital. When I began my research on Puneño migrant music in Lima in 1985, the Puno program *El Voz del Altiplano* (*The Voice of the* Altiplano, founded in 1980) on Radio Agricultura was my initial and constant source of information about the many Puneño musical events that happened each weekend, and the regional associations that sponsored them. Even in the 1980s the regional migrant groups were considered aliens in the city, and this program was advertised as being for the "*colonia Puneña en Lima*" (Puneño colony in Lima). Although companies hoping to reach migrant consumers would advertise on these programs, many of the shows were largely supported by the personal and regional club notices that were aired. Mass media such as radio have typically functioned to cater to and create mass audiences and masses of consumers; in Lima, however, commercial radio came to serve the grassroots interests of increasingly specific regional migrant "colonies." This inverse process was possible because of the number of highlanders in Lima but especially because of the strength of regional identity as the basis of people's sense of self and social networks. Highlanders from a particular region were attracted to the recordings and radio shows that were directed at them.

By the early 1980s, the *coliseos* had disappeared from the scene. Peruvian ethnomusicologist Josafat Roel told me that these venues went out of style because highlanders in Lima began to demand "more traditional" (i.e., less stylized) forms of highland music. Migrant musicians I spoke with said that the *coliseos* died because musicians were tired of performing without pay for the profit of the owners. By the 1980s, highland music from all regions of the country was going strong in Lima, but the contexts of performance shifted from venues owned by outsiders to events organized by the migrants themselves, especially through the auspices of regional clubs. During the 1960s, the music being recorded also began to shift to more indigenous styles in addition to the urban-country *wayno* performers. For example, Qhantati Ururi from Conima published a long-playing record of indigenous Aymara music (*sikuris, pitus, pinkillus*, etc.; see Chapter 1) with Odeon in 1965. Whereas in earlier decades elite Peruvians controlled the musical representations of "Andeanness" for nationalistic and commercial purposes, by the 1970s the migrants had reached a critical mass and so began to take control over their own musical activities, media outlets, and signs of identity. The migrant regional associations were at the center of this phenomenon.

HIGHLAND REGIONAL ASSOCIATIONS

When the first migrants from a particular rural region arrived in Lima, they had a very difficult time. They looked and spoke differently and faced social prejudice because of this. They did not know their way around. They typically did not have skills or education for work in the city and so could only land menial jobs, if they found employment at all. Coming from small villages and towns where they knew everyone, all of a sudden they knew no one and were very lonely. Some early migrants gave up and went home, but the more determined stayed and established a foothold in the city. As others from home arrived, they sought out these pioneers—often family members, friends, or friends of friends. They initially stayed with them and sought their help finding a job and their own place to live. Since they did not know anyone else, people from the same region hung out together—playing soccer, drinking, having parties, playing music, dancing—when they were not working. And so, community-based and regional social networks in the city evolved naturally among lower-class migrants.

Formal regional clubs or regional associations are found in cities throughout Latin America and Africa. Among lower-class rural migrants of indigenous and *mestizo* backgrounds, formal institutions often emerged organically out of the self-help networks described above. In Peru, however, there are elite social clubs that represent entire highland departments (e.g., Club Puno, Club Cusco), the members of which would self-identify as *criollo* or at least certainly *mestizo*. There are also associations representing ever smaller political–geographical units: from provinces to districts to specific towns and communities. Working-class migrant clubs tend to be at the more specific end of the continuum. The associations also vary widely from membership in the hundreds to associations with only twenty or thirty families.

In 1929 there were approximately forty-eight regional associations in Lima (Laos, 1929:283–290); by 1980 there were approximately six thousand (Altamirano, 1984:15)! This huge increase mirrors the demographic shift from the highlands to Lima. Yet most migrants did not join associations but rather tried to assimilate into *criollo* society, as Schaedel described. Other highlanders, however, decided that their best chance for social and economic advancement was to band together. Social networks are important for people of all classes, but for some

Andeans of peasant background the regional clubs were essential for social, economic, and psychological survival in the hostile environment of Lima.

The working-class associations from Conima that I studied in the mid-1980s were tight self-help networks that supplied child care for members, had a group cemetery plot, and developed cottage industries that employed members and their children as well as new Conimeños who arrived in the city. They had a fund to help members in times of medical and other kinds of emergencies. They also participated in a land invasion together with other highland migrants to establish the squatter settlement that ultimately became the officially recognized urban area of Mariano Melgar. Thus, the members of the club Centro Social Conima all lived together in the same neighborhood—surrounded by migrants from all over the highlands—and they helped each other build their houses. Like the members of regional associations throughout the city, home town—Conimeño—identity was the glue that held all this together. The first Conimeño club, Union Progresista Conima, had people from both indigenous and *mestizo* backgrounds, whereas Centro Social Conima members self-identified as being of indigenous extraction from the *ayllus*. Nonetheless, when returning to visit Conima after living for years in Lima, the migrants of Centro Social were identified by people at home as "*los Limeños*," and they looked and behaved like *mestizos* (Figure 4.2), illustrating the fluidity of these identity categories (Turino, 1993, chap. 10).

It is common for regional associations to organize religious festivals and music/dance events in the city, but in a number of cases, they hire or enlist the collaboration of "hometown" performers from outside the club ranks. The working-class clubs from Puno differ in that they perform the music and dances themselves. This had not always been the case. Before the mid-1970s, playing soccer (*futbol*) was the main social activity that brought Puneño club members together on a weekly basis. While some clubs, such as Union Progresista Conima, did perform hometown music together occasionally in private, soccer was the main public activity through which the club interacted with other regional associations. The Conima residents in Lima told me that initially they would have been ashamed to play indigenous music in the city publicly, afraid that people would laugh at them. These comments reflect the effects of Limeños' discriminatory attitudes toward highlanders and migrants' desires to deny their peasant background and assimilate into *criollo* society. Soccer was a safe activity in so far as it was not associated with any particular regional or "ethnic" heritage. After 1975,

FIGURE 4.2   *Centro Social Conima in downtown Lima.*

however, there was a major shift and performing panpipes and the other Conimeño wind instruments had become the major public focal activity for the three working-class Conimeño clubs in Lima. Why the change?

As noted earlier, the migrant flow from Puno was somewhat later than those from other highland regions, but by the 1970s there was a critical mass of working-class Puneños in the city—and there is power in numbers. In addition, Velasco's nationalist celebration of indigenous music and lifeways helped bolster Puneños' self-confidence and pride in themselves in the face of Limeño prejudice. At first, it was higher-class clubs, such as Asociacíon Juvenil Puno, that began to organize public events for Puneño music and dance in city parks and theaters. Following this lead, by the end of the 1970s, smaller working-class clubs came to realize that they could organize events themselves and that they could collect the entrance fees for the benefit of the association (no one would pay to watch soccer matches). This type of grassroots organizing by clubs from many regions effectively put the *coliseos* out of business by the early 1980s. Switching from soccer to music had another benefit. Hometown identity was the glue that held migrant self-help

FIGURE 4.3 *Centro Social Conima playing five-hole* pinkillus *and dancing* carnavales *in downtown Lima.*

networks together in the city; because of the specificity of community and regional styles, music/dance performance clearly communicated and celebrated that identity. A Conimeño migrant in Lima once told me "Conima is like our mother, and playing our music is like a portrait of mother."

Although the Conimeño clubs play *tarkas* and *pinkillus* during carnival season, they specialize in Conimeño *sikuri* (panpipe) music most of the year (Figure 4.3). Belonging to a network of regional clubs from the Province of Huancané, the Conimeño clubs organize a festival once a year and participate in their sister clubs' events, which are identical in form. As advertised on Radio Agricultura, club festivals are held on Sunday afternoons and through the evening in the walled-off playgrounds of local schools. The host club sells tickets at the door and beer and food at a separate table. The invited clubs begin arriving in the early afternoon and play informally in different parts of the playground as spectators, usually other folks from Huancané, arrive to listen to the music, eat, drink, and socialize. The main event of the festival is a "folklore contest," which begins mid-afternoon. In the Huancané club network, there were several contest categories, including *sikuris*, *sikumorenos* (a *mestizo* style of panpipe performance), costumed dances from Puno, and brass bands; each participating club specialized in one of these traditions. During the competition, the club ensembles perform three pieces in front of a table of judges and the spectators and are evaluated on the tightness of their sound, their choreography, and their costumes. Trophies are awarded the winners. In Peru, these "folklore contests" (*concursos folkloricos*) hail back to the original 1927 event sponsored by Leguía in Rimac and, following suit, transform participatory traditions into presentational ones during this portion of the festival. After the contest is over, the different groups perform for general dancing around the playground, and it is at this point that these urban events more closely resemble the participatory *fiestas* back home.

On the Sundays that Centro Social Conima is not participating in a festival, all the male members meet at the home of the *guía* (guide) of the musical ensemble for a rehearsal (Figure 4.4). For families that want to belong to the regional association, the male head of the household must be a member of the musical ensemble. Being a member of good standing in this voluntary association depends on consistent participation, and since musical performance and rehearsals are the group's main social activities, performing with the ensemble is basically mandatory. The Sunday rehearsals are also social events; the members talk and drink together during rest periods, but the main thrust is to learn and practice music. Some of the members confided to me that they were not particularly interested in playing music, but they wanted to belong to the association for all the practical reasons discussed earlier and, thus, were required to participate in the musical ensemble. Other members were enthusiastic about playing panpipes, and everyone was proud of their club's success in many festival contests. Conima had become widely known as a center for *sikuri* performance, so the

FIGURE 4.4 *Centro Social Conima rehearsing panpipes at a member's home in Mariano Melgar.*

Conimeño migrants took extra pride in performing the music from their hometown.

It is striking that many of the club members had not been interested in panpipe performance when they lived in Conima. Migrants are a self-selecting group who often were particularly attracted to the city by the promises of "modernity." As young people, their sights were set elsewhere and they were less inclined to participate in indigenous lifeways. Thus, the majority of Centro Social members learned to play Conimeño music in Lima. The few members who had performance experience before leaving home took on the roles of teachers and ensemble directors.

One musical goal of Centro Social Conima and the other working-class Conimeño clubs was to sound "just like they do in Conima." The other major goal was to hone their performance so that they could compete effectively in festival contests, thereby transforming a fully participatory tradition into a presentational mode of performance. In order to reach these goals, the club ensembles had to operate in a very different manner from the *ayllu* ensembles at home. Rather than the ad hoc, egalitarian style of *ayllu* ensemble organization, the club music directors took a very active, sometimes dictatorial role in telling people how to play and in arranging the music. On one occasion, I even heard a director tell an unskilled player to blow inaudibly so that he would not hurt the ensemble's sound in an upcoming contest. A *guía* could never have gotten away with such behavior in Conima (see Chapter 1). In *ayllu* ensemble rehearsals the night before a festival, the main activity is composing new pieces, and originality is highly valued in Conima. The regional clubs in Lima spend a good deal of rehearsal time copying cassette tapes of Conimeño groups that someone has brought them. They play the recordings over and over and attempt to match the performance precisely. Such strict imitation of another ensemble's style and repertory would be considered shameful in Conima, but the migrants consider it necessary if they are to "sound just like Conima." A club member once told me that because many of the members had lived at least half their lives in Lima, if they began composing music it would show new urban influences and they would "no longer sound like Conima." Thus, they opted for strict imitation (CD track 28).

ACTIVITY 4.4 *Compare CD track 28 by Centro Social Conima in Lima and track 2 by Qhantati Ururi of Conima, both of the same* sikuri lento *genre. Remembering that for indigenous Andeans subtle musical differences are recognized as important, listen carefully to the two tracks and write a few sentences describing the differences and similarities that you hear: "Track 28 'sounds like Conima' because . . . and sounds different from Qhantati because. . . ."*

Because the Conimeño migrant musicians are focused on presentational performance rather than merely playing in participatory events, their music tends to be tighter, more controlled, and neatly organized, as well as less spontaneous and varied. Centro Social's drumming tends to be stiffer than that of highland players, and the heterophonic edges that create density and interest in hometown music are rooted out. For presentational performance in general, and contest performance in particular, predictability, precision, and control of the artistic product become major values, whereas participatory music making in Conima is about *play* and *playfulness*; and these different orientations leave audible traces in the musical sound. Thus, although the migrant musicians were dedicated to imitating highland groups, they elected not to adopt the loose, playful quality of highland performance because it would have hurt them in festival competitions.

At a general level, the members of Centro Social have been successful at reproducing hometown musical style—creating a "portrait of mother"—but they have been able to do so because they have adopted different values and ways of operating compared to hometown musicians. Strict imitation rather than original creation, hierarchical control of ensemble musicians rather than an open egalitarian approach, and strict ordering and arranging of all musical details rather than a varied and spontaneous approach are prime examples. It is often said that migrants "brought their Andean music and culture with them when they moved to Lima." As the case of the Conimeño migrants shows, the situation is more complex than this. It might be more accurate to say that the migrants reproduced selected aspects of hometown music, mainly learned in the city, for specific reasons. They imitated the general sound style because it communicated their Conimeño identity and because the fame of Conimeño panpipe music garnered them prestige in migrant music circles. On the other hand, their musical values and approach to rehearsing and playing music were radically different from those in Conima. In terms of cultural continuity and change, which are more fundamental: values and practices or sound style?

Conimeño migrants did not merely "bring their culture with them"; rather, they created new combinations of values, practices, and style based on their needs, circumstances, and experiences in Lima. Most immigrant and diaspora communities forge new lifeways that draw on the values, models, and habits from both the original "homeland" as well as the new home. These creative combinations become even more pronounced for the children of immigrants, especially in situations where social prejudices block easy assimilation into the "host" society.

Such was the case with the children of Andean migrants in Lima during the twentieth century.

CHICHA MUSIC AND THE CHILDREN OF ANDEAN MIGRANTS

In the Conimeño regional clubs that I worked with, only one or two of the migrants' sons played panpipes with the ensemble, although all were welcome. The children attended family-oriented club events and the Sunday festivals but did not participate directly in the ensemble or organizational activities. The second generation, Lima-born children of highlanders, struggled with issues about their own identity. Many had little or no direct experience living in rural Andean communities and were not considered highlanders by their parents or themselves. Yet growing up in highland families, often in neighborhoods surrounded by other people from the sierra, they were not considered Limeños or *criollos* either. Several kids of Conimeño parents told me that they did not know where they belonged. Beginning in the 1960s, a new form of Peruvian popular music known as *chicha* (Andean corn beer) emerged that precisely articulated the ambiguous identity of second-generation Andeans in cities.

By the 1960s, a Colombian genre of dance music, the *cumbia*, had become popular in Lima, enjoyed by migrants as well as *criollos*. Played by urban dance bands or with other instrumentation, *cumbias* are in simple duple meter with a hallmark rhythmic ostinato played on a scrapper or shaker. Widely diffused throughout Latin America, highlanders considered the *cumbia* an urban, cosmopolitan genre. During the 1960s and 1970s, bands in Lima and other Peruvian cities began to combine the *cumbia* rhythm with *wayno* melodies played on electric guitars, bass, Caribbean percussion (*timbales*, congas, cowbell), and electric keyboards backing a lead singer. The eighth-two-sixteenth note *wayno* rhythm was easily adapted to the *cumbia* feel. For example, "Valicha," a popular *wayno* from Cusco, was performed as a *cumbia* by the proto-*chicha* band Los Destellos (hear CD tracks 29 and 30).

ACTIVITY 4.5 *Look up "cumbia" in the library or on the Internet and take out or download an example to listen to. Pay close attention to the rhythm in the percussion instruments and in the bass line, which are defining features of the genre.*

ACTIVITY 4.6   *Compare the two performances of "Valicha" on CD tracks 29 and 30. Besides the change in instrumentation, note the alterations in the phrasing of the melody.*

As *chicha* emerged in its own right, new songs were composed with lyrics predominantly about youthful love but also about the situation of Andean migrants in the city. One such song, by the famous *chicha* band of the 1980s Los Shapis, is "Ambulante Soy" (I am a street vendor), referring to the informal economy of untaxed commerce that exploded on the streets of Peruvian cities among migrants:

I am a street vendor.
I am a proletariat.
I am a street vendor.
I am a proletariat.

Selling shoes,
Selling food,
Selling jackets
Supporting my home.

One of the main goals of highland migrants in Lima was the advancement of their children through education, leading to professional employment. These shared class aspirations were again simply addressed in another Los Shapis song, "Somos Estudiantes" (CD track 31):

We are students
We are Peru
We are students
We are Peru

We are teachers
For our children.
Doctors we will be
For the orphans.
We are engineers
For our country.
We are architects
Of our destiny.
We are lawyers
Of the poor.

Chicha music communicated the complicated identity of second-generation migrants precisely through its combination of signs. The *wayno*-influenced melodies functioned as indices pointing to their highland heritage. The *cumbia* rhythm and Caribbean percussion stood for the urban, cosmopolitan part of their experience and identity. The rock-influenced use of electric guitars, bass, and keyboards was a sign of cosmopolitan youth culture, as were the myriad songs about adolescent love. Lyrics such as those for "Ambulante Soy" and many others expressed the lower-class position of *chicha* fans, just as "Somos Estudiantes" expressed their class-based aspirations for improvement. The power of music for articulating new, complex social identities is that these different musical signs can be combined into a single coherent whole—a single song—exactly paralleling the ways the different aspects of the second generation's identity was a combination of highland background, urban residence, lower-class standing, and youth within the whole of a single person. *Chicha* music was thus like an icon, or "portrait," of who these young people were; and it became extremely popular with this huge demographic. As one Puneño migrant told me in the mid-1980s,

> *Chicha* is the new wave of music among migrants in Lima. At one time it was the music of people like Pastorita Huaracina. Now many of the *provincianos* are no longer from the sierra [i.e., of the second generation], and they are not from the city either. *Chicha* has become popular because with it they can become involved with city music without having to give up the *wayno* totally. It helps them make the change from the sierra to the city.

Whereas the first generation of migrants in regional clubs remained primarily dedicated to the music of their home region in ever more specific terms, *chicha* music was popular with highlanders in general and during the 1980s and 1990s could serve as a pan-Andean common denominator. Thus, when banks or politicians wanted to appeal to migrants in general, they used *chicha* in their advertisements and rallies, rather than a regionally specific style that would attract only people from that place. Notice that in the second line of "Somos Estudiantes" Los Shapis sing "We are Peru." Whereas the urban *wayno* singers of an earlier era referenced specific places in their stage names, as did, logically, the regional clubs, Los Shapis billed themselves as "Los Shapis del Peru"; and *chicha* programs on Radio Agricultura addressed the "*pueblo Peruano*" (the Peruvian people).

In a way, *chicha* evoked a kind of return to the pan-Andeanism and national identification that was unsuccessfully propagated by some elite politicians and intellectuals of the 1920s, but there was a difference. This was the beginning of a grassroots articulation of national identification, not for political alliance with the state but because regionalism no longer made sense for the urban-born children and grandchildren of Andean migrants. Indeed, during the presidency of Alberto Fujimori (1990–2000) after 1990, the state remained as alien to the general Peruvian population as ever. But the idea of "Peru" filled an identity void left by the decline of regionalism among the progeny of highland migrants, and this huge demographic became an irresistible target for marketing and basis for generating new musical styles. It made good commercial sense for groups like Los Shapis and their record companies to seek and help build larger national markets, as opposed to the specific regional ones that *wayno* singers had appealed to formerly. Thus, unlike the usual nation-state linkage that is promoted by political nationalist discourse, this was a kind of default, as well as capitalist-inspired, national identification that largely side-stepped the state.

TECHNOCUMBIA

By the end of the twentieth century, something new was happening. Rural Andean migrants were not just heading to Lima and other major Peruvian cities but, in greater numbers, also immigrating to cities and countries around the world. In 2004, I visited my *compadres* in Conima to find that my goddaughter and her sister now lived in São Paulo, Brazil. The Conimeño wind ensembles described in Chapter 1 were still performing the same styles, but the best-known group in the district, Qhantati Ururi of *ayllu* Sulcata, was now traveling fairly regularly to La Paz, Bolivia, to record CDs. In this period of neoliberal economics and globalist discourse, people were moving farther afield, across country borders; and fueled by media corporations, musical influences were circulating widely as well.

During the Fujimori period, a new trend in Peruvian popular music known as *technocumbia* developed from the roots of *chicha*. Peruvian scholars Raul Romero and Víctor Vich observe several general differences between *chicha* and *technocumbia*. Whereas *chicha* bands were typically fronted by male vocalists, young, attractive female singing stars have a prominent place in *technocumbia*. *Chicha* was produced for lower- and working-class migrant audiences and typically scorned by upper-class Limeños, whereas, according to Romero *technocumbia* is enjoyed by people across class boundaries. Finally, while *chicha* was a fairly homogenous blending of highland *wayno* with urban *cumbia*, Caribbean percussion, and electric instruments, Romero and Vich argue that *technocumbia* artists emphasize the urban *cumbia* and downplay Andean elements.

In keeping with neoliberal-era commodity flows, I would suggest that a major characteristic of *technocumbia* is ecclectism—it includes musical signs and influences from many countries and genres, including highland Peru and *chicha* itself. The most constant feature of the style is the use of *cumbia* rhythm, although groups associated with *technocumbia* will do pieces in other rhythms as well. Additional typical features are the use of synthesizers and studio recording techniques, especially heavy reverb and compression, which create a glossy, punchy pop sound. The texts are usually about romantic love, dancing, and partying—this is party music.

Beyond these commonalities, individual artists creatively combine a variety of elements. For example, "Tic, Tic, Tac," by the group Joven Sensacíon (Young Sensation, CD track 32) begins with a funk drum riff, bass line, and hip hop scratching to accompany rap-like vocal delivery. This segues immediately to a synthesized panpipe sound rendering a pentatonic melody reminiscent of 'Andean folkloric music' (see Chapter 5) and a square drum rhythm; synthesized trumpets begin to echo the panpipe line. Twenty-three seconds into the song there is a very short rest and the band shifts to playing a *cumbia* with the melody on synthesizer and fuzz-tone electric guitar for the first pass and to (real) trumpets, à la a salsa band, on the second. Then, two young, fairly nondescript, soft male voices alternate on the first and second verses about a young girl in the neighborhood whom the protagonist is in love with. The two vocalists sing the chorus together: "*Tic Tic Tac, Tic Tic Tac, es el sonido de mí corazón*" (is the sound of my heart), *tic tic tac, tic tic tac, cuando la veo pasar*" (when I see her walk by). All this (including the same text) repeats a second time, beginning with the panpipe melody. The recording concludes with a fuzz-tone electric guitar solo, a trumpet solo, a rap-like vocal section over percussion accompaniment reminiscent of *samba-reggae* from Brazil, and finally the two vocalists singing the "Tic Tic Tac" chorus into a fade out.

If the different elements of *chicha* clearly indexed highlands/city/youth/class for second-generation migrants in Lima, the multiple elements of this *technocumbia* piece just as clearly index a new cosmopolitan subjectivity and youth culture that can comfortably combine funk, hip hop, "Andean folkloric music," salsa, *cumbia*, *samba-reggae*, rock guitar, and pop vocals—all within a three-minute, forty-two-second piece! The massive recording and media corporations have made all these sounds, and many more, part of the habitual soundscape of young people in many places, and it is only natural that they would begin to use them in their own music. The same eclecticism packed into this one song is also evident across the work of different performers associated with *technocumbia*.

Meanwhile in Peru, Conimeños are still performing *tarkas* for carnival (CD track 1). Dance dramas, like those described for Paucartambo, are still being vibrantly performed throughout the country. New commercial *wayno* singers such as Sonia Morales from Ancash can still be heard in buses and on the radio throughout the highlands. For Morales and other contemporary *wayno* singing stars, specific regional associations are not as important as they once were. To expand their markets, they attempt to appeal to highlanders across regions—Morales is accompanied by harp rather than Ancash string band and was popular in Cusco and Puno during my visit in 2004.

There are also Peruvian *chicha*, rock, salsa, and jazz bands, as well as revivalist Afro-Peruvian music/dance ensembles (see Feldman, 2006), *vals criollo* duos, and classical orchestras. The chronological description of Andean music in Lima presented in this chapter is not meant to suggest that as new styles emerged old ones disappeared. True, *chicha* is not as big as it was in the 1980s, but what seems to be the case for Peru generally is that new styles and approaches to music making simply get added to existing styles, enhancing the overall richness of Peruvian musical life.

CHAPTER 5

Andean Music in the Cities of the World

In 1976, I heard a recording of Andean music for the first time; it was one of those chance experiences that changed the course of my life, although I did not fully realize it at the time. I was living in Brattleboro, Vermont, taking music classes in preparation for graduate school during the day and working on the acute schizophrenic ward of a local psychiatric hospital at night. I was burned out and needed a change. The music on the recording was so beautiful, so moving, that I decided to take time off and travel to its source. I had a little money saved and had already determined to become an ethnomusicologist. So, armed with high school Spanish and with Bruno Nettl's *Theory and Method in Ethnomusicology* (1964) and Alan Merriam's *The Anthropology of Music* (1964) in my backpack, in 1977 I set off for Cusco, Peru, to try fieldwork and learn about this music first hand. Getting off the plane and seeing the colonial red-tiled roofs of Cusco against the green rainy-season mountains, I remember thinking "This is it," and it was, although not in the ways I expected.

The recording I had heard back in Vermont was *Urubamba* by the group of the same name (1974, Colombia Records KG 32896). It featured *kena* solos by Argentine virtuoso Uña Ramos. His playing fluctuated between the deep, rich, mysterious sounds of the larger flutes he plays and fluid, purer sounds in the higher octaves. A large single-row panpipe was also used as a lead instrument on some of the tracks and in airy counter melodies behind the *kena* for variety. With fast glissando and vibrato, the panpipe player sounded more like European panpipe star Zamfir than an Andean performer. The winds were accompanied by nylon-stringed *charango*, described in the liner notes as the most "native" of South American stringed instruments. The *charango* is used for strumming diatonic chords; for delicate, scintillating, plucked arpeggiated chords; or to play the melody in alternation with the flute or in unison with it. Rounding out the quartet, a guitar was used for playing bass lines and strumming, and the Argentinean drum known as *bombo* accented the rhythms.

This instrumental album includes a variety of moods and genres. There are upbeat pieces in *wayno* and *cueca* (6/8 *marinera*-like) rhythms, such as "Kachapari" and "Urubamba," respectively. "Kachapari" (leave taking; CD track 33) consists of a short melody in basic AABB *wayno* form that is repeated over and over (review CD tracks 14, 15, 25). The Urubamba ensemble creates a sense of contrast and progression by first presenting the simple *wayno* melody with solo *kena* in the low register for the A sections and in the higher register for the B sections against the homophonic strings. On the third repetition of the melody, the *kenista* moves to the higher octave for both the A and B sections and a second *kena*, playing in parallel thirds, is added on the B sections. The tempo increases and the strumming intensifies for the fourth repetition played by the two *kenistas* in the higher octave. Thus, in spite of the simplicity of the basic musical material, carefully orchestrated contrasts and a sense of development and excitement are created, which are so important in presentational and recorded musics.

The pieces on the album that really fired my imagination at the time of my initial hearing were the slower mysterious ones such as "El Eco" ("The Echo") and "Campanas de Santa Cruz" ("Bells of Santa Cruz," translated in the liner notes as "Death in Santa Cruz"). In "Campanas de Santa Cruz" (CD track 34), mystery is created by the timbre of the wind instruments themselves as well as the ambiguous rhythm and harmony. Performed in the key of G minor, this piece opens with a drone-like introduction on the tonic minor chord. The chord progression moves romantically between minor and major tonalities: i . . . . //: i IV i IV i IV i . . . . III VI v i . . . . :// (the use of the major IV was also an effective touch). Although the tempo is relatively slow, the rhythm provides its own ambiguity and tension with the drum and guitar bass line playing a repeated ostinato in 3/4 meter (quarter, quarter rest, two eighths), with the *charango* repeating a *vidala* rhythm in 6/8 over the 3/4 pattern (*vidala* is an Argentine genre resembling the Peruvian *yaraví*). The *kena* takes the main lyrical melody. In the sections where the minor tonic chord is held for a series of measures, the panpipe plays evocative arch-shaped gestures, creating a sense of movement over harmonic stasis and the rhythmic insistence of the drum. For the most part, the music on the album is homophonic and transparent, each instrument clearly audible.

In many ways, Urubamba's music was similar to other acoustic music I enjoyed; but upon first hearing, I was struck by the exotic differences in the quality of the instrumental timbres, the melodies, the romantic and ambiguous harmonies, and the infectious *wayno* and 6/8 rhythms. In fact, it *was* music I had heard before. In 1970, Simon and Garfunkel released the song "El Condor Pasa" ("I'd rather be a hammer than a nail") on their hit album *Bridge Over Troubled Waters*. Urubamba, based in Paris and formerly known as Los Incas, played the background track for the Simon and Garfunkel hit, and it was Paul Simon who produced Urubamba's 1974 album that sent me to Peru.

Imagine my surprise as I began exploring the different music scenes in Cusco to discover that very little of the music there had much to do with the sounds on the Urubamba recording. As mentioned in Chapter 2, I met Julio Benavente early on, and his music did not sound like Urubamba. Each day I passed a pair of blind street musicians who played *kena* and harp, and this flautist's thin, wispy sound bore little resemblance to Uña Ramos's rich, round *kena* tone. I went to Paucartambo and other festivals and heard wispy, vibratoless *kenas* combined with densely played violins, accordions, and harps—not crisp guitar and *charango*; the textures/timbres of the Cusqueño *orquestas* were dense and heterophonic and radically different from anything I had ever heard. Blasting from radios in the market, on buses, and in neighborhood stores I heard the commercial *wayno* singers like Pastorita Huaracina. In hindsight, and in comparison to indigenous and rural *mestizo* performers, the urban *wayno* stars sound polished and presentational; but upon first encounter, the women's high-pitched nasal voices and the songs themselves sounded weird—radically different from any music I knew at that time.

Urubamba recorded in New York. The liner notes for the album are by band member J. Milchberg, who claims all the pieces as his own compositions or collaborations with bandmates J. Huirse and Uña Ramos. Milchberg romantically explains "Urubamba is a river from Peru which winds at the foot of Machu Picchu, the last fortified city of the Incas. The Urubamba group chose this name to carry the culture of the Incas beyond all frontiers, as would an open river." The picture on the front cover of the album captures the quartet on stage wearing colorful Andean ponchos and belts. Three of the musicians have shoulder-length hair, and three are bearded; one wears denim overalls, which were popular in the "back-to-the-land" hippie movement of the time.

The Urubamba River runs near Cusco, down the "Sacred Valley of the Incas" past Machu Picchu; but the Incas are long gone, and the sound of this Paris-based ensemble had no presence in the local Cusco scene, with one exception. There was a group of university students who had formed a band known as Arco Iris (Rainbow). This combo of *kena* soloist backed by *charango*, guitar, and bombo closely mirrored Urubamba's style. They played local *waynos* as well as pieces from Bolivia, Argentina, Chile, and elsewhere, the latter often learned from recordings. Arco Iris performed in upscale restaurants for tourists as well as for local university students and hippies. The Urubamba recording and others like it could also be heard in tourist shops, restaurants, and hotels that catered to foreign visitors. It was Urubamba's "folkloric" style, rather than Cusqueño *orquestas*, Pastorita Huaracina, Benavente's *charango*, Conimeño *siku* ensembles, or Los Shapis's *chicha* music, that cosmopolitans around the world had come to associate with the Andes and the capital of the Incas.

How did this happen? Where and how did the "folkloric" style of groups like Urubamba originate? It was certainly not native to Cusco or Peru, although it featured instruments diffused throughout Peru and Bolivia and emphasized Peruvian/Incan imagery, much like the *indigenistas* had done. Similar to the *indigenista* intellectuals of the 1920s, the performers and fans of Andean folkloric music pertained to a different cultural formation from the indigenous and *mestizo* musicians that groups like Urubamba alluded to. Andean folkloric music is not so much *Andean* as it is an Andean-inspired component of the modernist-cosmopolitan cultural formation. Let me try to explain what I mean.

COSMOPOLITANISM AS A TYPE OF CULTURAL FORMATION

Largely because of the effects of nationalist discourse, people are in the habit of thinking of different cultures as belonging to particular countries—by "culture" I mean socially transmitted lifeways that are based on shared habits of thought and practice. But as we have seen for Peru, there are frequently a variety of contrasting cultural groups residing within the borders of a particular country. There are also *cultural formations* (people related through prominent sets of shared habits of belief, thought, technology use, practices, etc.) that are not place-specific but that are found among particular groups of people across the borders of different countries around the world. *Cosmopolitanism* is one type of translocal cultural formation. Although often thinking of themselves as unattached "citizens of the world," cosmopolitans tend to congregate with each other in particular sites around the world—in particular cities such as New York, Paris, Boulder, and Brattleboro, as well as in more specific sites such as universities, jazz clubs, "folk" clubs, and opera houses. Like the members of any cultural group, cosmopolitans tend to congregate because they share habits of thought and practice that make communication and social intercourse more comfortable, indeed possible.

The people involved with many cosmopolitan formations tend to celebrate eclecticism. That is, cosmopolitans soak up ideas, practices, and technologies from anywhere in the formation and tend to value this "worldly knowledge" of different languages, cuisines, technologies, clothing, art, and music styles. This is not to say that anything goes. Like any cultural formation, specific cosmopolitan formations are identifiable and made coherent by prominent habits of thought, value, belief, and practice. As Max Weber described long ago, the modernist-cosmopolitan cultural formation—the one to which 'Andean folkloric music' pertains—is identifiable by a belief in technological "progress," scientific method, capital accumulation, occupational specialization, and "rational" bureaucratic organization and control.

These foundational beliefs and values shape other realms of life, such as music making. Thus, in the modernist formation, 'rationally' planned (rehearsed) and controlled presentational performance by set, organized, specialized ensembles is valued more highly than the messy, unpredictable quality of participatory performance. At a more specific level, textural clarity is an index of 'rational' control just as virtuosic solos *index* (both communicate and are the product of) high specialization. When the cosmopolitan value of eclecticism—say, an interest in exotic Andean music and imagery—is combined with the fundamental modernist values, the result is the transformation, or 'reform,' of the original tradition in light of modernist values.

On "Kachapari," Urubamba performs a simple *wayno* tune with "native" Andean instruments, and they refer to it as "Inca" (read "indigenous") music. When indigenous Andean music is played in participatory settings, however, the same melody is repeated over and over for a long time without planned contrasts or development, except for concluding *fuga* sections (e.g., CD tracks 1–8). Lengthy, undifferentiated repetition is, in fact, important to participatory music because it allows easy access for musicians who are not highly rehearsed and helps people get in, and stay in, social synchrony with other community members for extended periods of time (see Chapter 1). On "Kachapari," Urubamba adds planned contrasts and a progressive sense of development (CD track 33). This approach is effective for creating interest and excitement in presentational settings and on recordings where the audience is not playing the music or dancing. At a deeper level, Urubamba's emphasis on musical contrast and development also may be the result of their own modernist values favoring "progress" and change. Whatever the case, in Andean folkloric music, instruments and genres that pertain to unspecialized village participatory performance are adopted for professional concert presentation and high-fidelity recording and undergo major stylistic transformations in the process.

Here is the punch line: Urubamba-styled 'folkloric music' is the type most associated with the Andean region by cosmopolitans because it was a modernist-cosmopolitan style from its inception. But there is another point that needs clarification. Beyond the value of eclecticism, why would modernists take such an interest in "pre-modern Inca" music?

Embedded within cultural formations there are many more specific identity groups or *cultural cohorts*—people who both share the habits of the broader formation as well as self-identify more specifically according to particular traits, interests, beliefs, and values (Turino, 2008). Within the modernist-cosmopolitan formation during the 1960s and 1970s (and still today), there was an *antimodernist cohort* that became engaged with indigenous and rural-based musics. The members of this cohort idealized the simplicity of rural community as an antidote to the stresses of their own 'modern' lives, and 'folk music' was an attractive icon of this idealization. Thus, locally distinctive yet directly related 'folk revivals' sprang up almost simultaneously among cosmopolitans in different sites around the world—Paris, New York, London, La Paz (Bolivia), Santiago (Chile), San Francisco, Boulder, Brattleboro, and many other places.

The members of this cohort, and I count myself among them, both had been deeply socialized from childhood with core modernist attitudes and then began to adopt alternative values by association with others in the antimodernist cohort. For the members of this cohort, the simplicity of Andean flutes and the "Kachapari" tune were as important to its meaning as Urubamba's artful development of the piece; long hair, beards, and wearing denim overalls on a formal concert stage reinforced the same mixture of signs and messages. This mixture—of artistic specialization and development with 'folk' simplicity—was the result of competing value systems within the same individuals who were both modernists and antimodernists at the same time. It was no accident that I encountered Urubamba in Brattleboro, Vermont—a folkie, hippie haven—in 1976 and was captivated by it. This music was designed for people like me by people like me. At the inception of the 'Andean folkloric style' during the 1950s, however, these people were not in Brattleboro or Cusco but, rather, in other modernist-cosmopolitan enclaves on the Left Bank of Paris and in Buenos Aires.

FROM BUENOS AIRES AND PARIS TO THE CITIES OF THE WORLD

Unlike the two other major types of translocal cultural formations—diasporas and *immigrant communities*—cosmopolitans do not claim an original homeland as the source and bedrock of social identity (see Chapter 4 for the case of the Conimeño immigrant community). Likewise the place of origin of cosmopolitan technologies and cultural practices—eating potatoes, using money, the radio, the automobile, e-mail—is largely irrelevant to their significance; rather, they are "of the modern world" and by now belong to anyone. While they do not claim homelands, specific cosmopolitan formations do have loci or power centers; and for the modernist formation, Paris was certainly a cultural power center throughout much of the twentieth century.

The (first) *tango* craze swept the modernist formation not from Buenos Aires but indirectly via Paris; for example, Vernon and Irene Castle learned the dance there and diffused it throughout the United States from New York (another locus) in the early twentieth century. The popularity of black music and arts during the 1920s and 1930s in Paris affected the legitimacy of jazz, the Cuban *son*, and Afro-Brazilian music among cosmopolitans in their home countries as well as elsewhere (Vianna, 1999; Moore, 1997:171–182; Rios, n.d.:2). French interest in the "exotic" and the "primitive" led to one of the first major studies of Andean music, *La Musique des Incas et Ses Survivances* (*Inca Music and Its Survivals*) by Marguerite and Raoul d'Harcourt in 1925. And Paris was a mecca for cosmopolitan Latin American composers, such as the Peruvian Teodoro Valcárcel who presented his *indigenista* work *Cuatro Canciones Incaicas* (*Four Inca Songs*) there in 1930 (Béhague, 1979:168).

Fernando Rios, the leading authority on Andean folkloric music, traces the creation of the style to Buenos Aires and especially Paris, both cosmopolitan cultural centers. In Buenos Aires during the 1940s, the Abalos Brothers performed Andean music and opened two Quechua-named clubs, Peña Achalay and Peña Achalay Huasi, in an upper-class neighborhood (*"peña"* came to refer to café/nightclub settings where 'folk music' was performed). The members of the Abalos Brothers came from elite family backgrounds in the northern, Andean sector of the country and helped popularize Andean music in the Argentine capital alongside the *tango* and the *gaucho*, which were central to Argentine national imagery. Rios describes the Abalos Brothers' live performances as including a segment entitled "Folklore of the Andes" (note the elite use of the term "folklore" here to refer to the musical practices of other cultural groups). Rios remarks "In this part of the show, the siblings played *bailecitos, yaravis* and *carnavalitos* [Argentine version of the *wayno*] with Andean *kenas* and *charangos*, standard guitars, and an Argentine *bombo . . .*" He concludes that the "*kena–charango*–guitar–*bombo* lineups in the style of Los Hermanos Abalos would become the standard among Andean folkloric groups in Bolivia, Chile, Mexico, France, Japan and many other sites beginning in the 1960s and 1970s" (n.d.:5–6). Indeed, Arco Iris had just this lineup during the mid to late 1970s in Cusco.

In 1951, the Paraguayan group Los Guaranís arrived in Paris with an Argentine music and dance company directed by a Spanish choreographer for theater presentations. Included in their performance was "a three-movement 'Peruvian Suite' (Yaraví, Huayño, Kachapampa War Dance), a sketch titled 'Indians in Saturday's Fair' evocatively set in the city of the Incas [Cuzco]" (Rios, n.d.:4). The cosmopolitan makeup of this artistic collaboration of Argentines, Paraguayans, and a Spanish director is important to note. Around 1955, Argentine *kena* player Carlos Ben-Pott (also a 'Dixieland' jazz clarinetist) formed the group Los Incas in Paris with the Argentine jazz bassist Ricardo Galeazzi, who played *charango* and second *kena*, and Venezuelan singers/guitarists/percussionists Elio Riveros and Narciso Debourg. Directly influenced by the Abalos Brothers, Los Incas played music from all over Latin America but specialized in the Andean pieces that the Abalos Brothers had made famous in Buenos Aires (Rios, n.d.:6). In 1958 in Paris, *kenista* Ricardo Galeazzi split off from Los Incas to form L'Ensemble Achalay (probably named after the Abalos's *peña*) to record the album *Musique Indienne des Andes* (*Indian Music of the Andes*). Urubamba's *charango* player and chief composer, Jorge Milchberg, was also a member of L'Ensemble Achalay. Milchberg had come to Paris to study classical music. He told Fernando Rios that he learned *charango* in France in order to support himself (2005:421). Unlike Los Incas' pan-Latin American repertory on their first album, L'Ensemble Achalay

only presented Andean repertory from Argentina, Bolivia, Ecuador and Peru. With Galeazzi's solo *kena* in the lead role on every track, this album contained perhaps the first European recording of the soon-to-be ubiquitous *El Condor Pasa*. On this album, Galeazzi played with Argentine *charanguista* Jorge Milchberg (a classically-trained pianist who later joined *Los Incas*), Italian singer/guitarist Romano Zanotti (who was raised in Argentina) and Marcello Bellandi.

Strikingly, the members of *Los Incas* and *L'Ensemble Achalay* learned to play Andean music in France—not in South America—while jamming at *L'Escale* (The Stopover), a cozy, wood-paneled local in Paris's bohemian Left Bank. . . . (Rios, n.d.:7)

Following the early commercial successes of these pioneer groups, there was a veritable explosion of 'Andean flute music' ensembles and recordings in Paris, and these artists began to tour Europe, popularizing the style more widely.

In 1963, Los Incas recorded a rearranged version of "El Condor Pasa" on their album *Amérique du Sud* that was soon to become the standard. The basic musical material for "El Condor Pasa" was created by Peruvian *indigenista* art music composer Daniel Alomía Robles as part of a music drama (a *zarzuela*) that debuted in Lima in 1913 and was a huge hit. The plot of the drama revolved around a Peruvian miners' fight against a Yankee imperialist mine owner; the condor served as an emblem of freedom. As an early example of *indigenismo*, Alomía was interested in highland Peruvian music; and the basic theme of "El Condor Pasa" was probably based on, or at least inspired by, existing Peruvian tunes. Following the success of Alomía's *zarzuela*, the song (re?)entered the popular music repertory. The street *kena*–harp duo that I passed every day in Cusco in 1977 played this song regularly. Once while walking in a remote rural area in the Department of Cusco in 1982, I was stopped by police. Thinking that I might be a spy or a terrorist, they roughly questioned me as to what I was doing there. When I told them that I was studying Peruvian music, they replied "Yeah, well can you play 'Condor Pasa'?" at which point I whipped out my *kena* and played the tune. Satisfied, they let me go. The song had become emblematic of Peruvian music at home as well as generally of Andean music abroad. Rios notes that Alomía's piano arrangement of "El Condor Pasa" was included in Xavier Cugat's 1938 edited volume *The Other Americas: Album of Typical Central and South American Songs and Dances*, which also included "the Cuban-inspired *La Conga Pasa* (!) and *The Mexican Hat Dance*" (Rios, n.d.:16). Spanish-born Cugat was a bandleader who came to the United States via Cuba and was one of the major popularizers of Latin American music for mainstream North American audiences. Thus, "El Condor Pasa" had already entered the cosmopolitan repertory of Latin American "classics" before the 1950s–1960s Paris boom.

In the mid-1960s, Paul Simon was staying in Paris, and he might have heard a popular French singer's vocal version of the song that was a hit on the radio. Rios remarks that around this time Los Incas' "*Charango* player Jorge Milchberg gave an *Amérique du Sud* album as a gift to the yet unknown North American Musician (Jorge Milchberg, p.c.). Enamored with this music, Simon added English lyrics to *El Cóndor Pasa* and recorded this version with Art Garfunkel—dubbed over *Los Incas'* track from *Amérique du Sud*" (Rios, n.d.:17). And so, North American 'folk music' and folk-rock fans were introduced to the mysterious sounds of Andean flutes via Buenos Aires, Paris, and Paul Simon; North Americans can still hear the tune regularly on oldies stations and while shopping in the supermarket.

> **ACTIVITY 5.1** *Do a Web search for "El Condor Pasa," investigating the different recorded versions and other information about the song. Download different recorded versions including that by Simon and Garfunkel.*

In summary to this point, as the cosmopolitan folkloric style emerged in the 1950s, it was defined by ensembles of one or two *kenas* played with vibrato, a round tone, and virtuosic display as the lead melody instrument; nylon-string *charango* used to strum harmonic support as well as pluck solos; nylon-string guitar used primarily as strummed harmonic accompaniment and for bass runs; and Argentinean *bombo*, a medium-sized drum with two goat- or calf-skin heads played with padded mallets or a mallet and stick. Much later in the history of the style, solo performance on single- and then double-row panpipes (i.e., one person rather than the usual two played the two rows) and other indigenous instruments were added to provide variety. Pieces were played instrumentally or with vocals. The pan-Latin American trait of parallel thirds was used for vocal or instrumental duos.

The imagery on album covers, group names (Los Incas, Urubamba), and costumes emphasized indigenous Andeans; and the repertory revolved around Andean music—*waynos* (CD tracks 14, 15, 25) *cuecas* (a Bolivian/Chilean version of the *marinera,* CD track 17), *yaravís* (CD track 16), and *vidalas* (an Argentine genre like the *yaraví*)—but also included songs from elsewhere in Latin America, including *zambas* and *gatos* from Argentina, *joropos* from Venezuela, and famous songs like "La Bamba" from Mexico. The repertory itself, then, was cosmopolitan, including some of the best-known Latin American songs and genres. The music was performed in 'folk' clubs and on concert stages. In stark contrast to the participatory music it alluded to, the Andean folkloric style thus emphasized textural clarity, musical contrasts, and soloistic performance, in keeping with these values in most modernist presentational musics. In the Andean folkloric style, contrasts were sometimes created by shifting tempos and meters (as in the classic "El Condor Pasa"), but the typical way was through different instruments taking the melodic lead on the basic melody of the song. Again, unlike the open-ended forms of participatory music, folkloric ensembles arranged their pieces in closed symmetrical forms around planned contrasts in the style of most modernist-cosmopolitan popular songs. If vocals were involved, the form might be instrumental intro/sung verse/*kena* solo/ sung verse/*charango* solo/sung verse or, if an instrumental, *kena* solo on melody/*kena* melody/*charango* solo on melody/*kena* melody. As other Andean instruments were added to the mix, they were fit into such alternation schemes as well as used for other types of contrast—e.g., a *kena*–panpipe duo in harmony for one repetition of the melody.

"ANDEAN FOLKLORIC MUSIC" IN THE ANDES

The cosmopolitan 'folk' clubs of the Left Bank of Paris were the launching pad for "Andean folkloric music" in Europe and the United States as well as in Latin American countries. If we think of culture simply in national terms, it seems ironic that musicians in the Andean countries would take their lead from the Paris scene. But if we think in terms of a cosmopolitan cultural formation—widely diffused in different countries but unified by similar habits of value, thought, and practice as well as by actual people traveling among the different cosmopolitan sites—then this situation makes sense. For example, the legendary Chilean political singer–songwriter Violeta Parra heard Los Incas' music in a Left Bank folk club in 1955, and Rios suggests that this was, perhaps, her first encounter with Andean folkloric music. She returned to Paris in 1962 with her children Angel and Isabel, where they tried to eke out a living performing for the next three years. Inspired by the popularity of Andean folkloric music, Parra encouraged her son Angel and her Swiss boyfriend, Gilbert Favre (a clarinetist), to learn the *kena*.

Not meeting with much success in Paris, however, the Parras and Favre returned to Santiago, Chile, where they opened their own folk club (La Peña de los Parra) and where Angel recorded one of the first Andean folkloric music albums in Chile (Rios, n.d.:11–12). The Parras' leftist politics and musical activism put them at the center of cultural–political life during the Salvador Allende presidential campaign and short-lived presidency. They also inspired other university musicians to incorporate the Andean folkloric style into what became known as the Chilean *nueva canción* (new song, new political song) movement with groups such as Quilapayún (founded in 1965) and Inti-Illimani (1967). Whereas Andean folkloric music was not particularly connected to political activism in Paris initially, *kenas, charangos,* and panpipes began to be associated with leftist, liberation politics among cosmopolitans due to the use of these instruments by *nueva canción* performers. This association became particularly strong after Allende was assassinated and groups such as Quilapayún and Inti-Illimani were driven into exile in Europe, where they toured widely.

Meanwhile, Swiss *kena* player Gilbert Favre had moved to La Paz, Bolivia, where in 1966 he founded Peña Naira with Bolivian art gallery owner Luis Ballón. Rios remarks that *Peña Naira* was the first "folkloric music" venue in La Paz, where formerly nightclubs featuring jazz, Latin dance bands, and striptease shows were the rule (2005:519–521). Favre played his *kena* and arranged to have panpipe troupes and other local indigenous and urban *mestizo* musicians perform during the opening weeks of his folk club. Previously, the La Paz elite would have had little interest in their country's "native" music; but in this context, supported by a local radio commentator and spearheaded by a European, Peña Naira became a huge success.

Favre also founded the prototypical Bolivian folkloric music ensemble in the Paris mold: Los Jairas (The Lazy Boys) with Bolivian *charango* virtuoso Ernesto Cavour, guitarist Julio Godoy, and, ultimately, singer/*bombo* player Edgar Yayo Joffré. Beginning as an ad hoc group for performances at Peña Naira, this ensemble went on to set the standard and popularize the Andean folkloric style in Bolivia through recordings and festival and nightclub performances. Many other young urban Bolivian musicians formed similar groups after the late 1960s and developed their own highly stylized approaches to Andean folkloric music. During peaks of popularity, bands like Savia Andina and Los Kjarkas dominated the airwaves in Bolivia and extended the style in different directions. Riding the 1990s' wave of Afrocentrism in cosmopolitan 'world music' circles, Los Kjarkas had a commercial hit with a 'folkloric' version of the Afro-Bolivian *saya* genre (originally performed with drums and participatory singing); the Peruvian group Yawar's cover of the Beatles hit "Michelle"—played with panpipe, *kena, charango*, and guitar—is another example of the possibilities.

The folkloric style also was widely adopted in Ecuador, where it began to take on local style features and genres such as the *sanjua-nito* (Ecuadorian correlate of the *wayno*). In fact, by the 1990s bands from Otavalo and other Ecuadorian regions had begun traveling the world to sell their crafts and CDs and perform music on the streets, in subways, and in festivals (Meisch, 2002). These musicians are commonly encountered in cosmopolitan sites performing *kenas*, panpipes, and *charangos* in "karaoke fashion," accompanied by prerecorded tracks blasting through their mobile PA systems. In Peru, the folkloric style has been somewhat less influential. It is widely performed in tourist locations, and there are *peñas* (nightclubs) for upper-middle-class urbanites where it is featured. A more interesting development is the blending of the folkloric style, repertoire, and instruments (e.g., electric *charango*) with rock instrumentation (electric guitars, bass, synthesizers, and drums) by such groups as Cusco's Pueblo Andino. This type of rock–folkloric fusion is common among young musicians throughout the Andean region.

Unlike anywhere else in the world, however, the folkloric style is so prominent in Bolivia that it has become the preeminent national emblem and popular commercial music. In spite of the facts that the folkloric style derived from cosmopolitan roots in Buenos Aires and Paris and was largely initiated in Bolivia by a European, Bolivians could claim special ownership of it since it featured instruments and certain genres indigenous to their country. It is also a common occurrence that the musical styles adopted as national emblems at home are the very ones that are well-known and valued in cosmopolitan circles abroad, thereby increasing local cosmopolitans' pride in their "national culture." Parallel cases are abundant and include *tango* for Argentina, *samba* for Brazil, the *son* for Cuba, the steelband for Trinidad, *mbira* music for Zimbabwe, *merengue* for the Dominican Republic, *mariachi* for Mexico, and jazz for the United States, among others.

As the folkloric style developed in Bolivia, it followed another trajectory that is typical of 'folkloric' music and 'folk revivals' elsewhere. Many of the first Bolivian ensembles were firmly in the cosmopolitan Buenos Aires–Parisian mold. The smooth, polished, virtuosic style of performance and eclectic repertory was attractive to Bolivian cosmopolitans because they shared the same musical values that gave rise to the style in the first place; i.e., they were part of the same cultural formation. Yet, as typically happens in cosmopolitan 'folk revivals' and 'world music' circles, attraction to a new or exotic style will lead certain people to search out increasingly distinctive *roots* styles that are alluded to in the cosmopolitan versions. In the United States, for example, "folkies" of the 1960s who were originally attracted to the music by polished professional groups like Peter, Paul, and Mary and the Kingston Trio sometimes began to search out and emulate "roots" blues and country performers who had served as sources for the "folk" popularizers. Likewise in the 1980s, some 'world music' fans who were first introduced to South African music through Paul Simon's hit LP *Graceland* went on to find recordings by the original African artists, and a dedicated few were even inspired to travel to the music's source.

Similarly, fueled by nationalist discourse and a search for 'authentic' Bolivian roots, already in 1968 Mario Gutiérrez and Agustín Mendieta formed the group Los Ruphay after having taken several trips to rural communities to experience indigenous music in its original setting. Their first recording of 1969 bore the English title "Folk Music of Bolivia" to appeal to tourists and included *siku*, *tarka*, and *pinkillu* pieces in the indigenous large-ensemble format, rare for folkloric musicians at the time (Rios, 2005:608). Over the next decades in Bolivia, other groups expanded the *kena–charango–bombo*–guitar quartet to include more indigenous instruments and more indigenous styles of performance in a variety of ways. For example, by the late 1980s, the Bolivian ensemble Grupo Aymara would do one concert set in the folkloric format and then a second set in indigenous style—only performing panpipes together accompanied by drums or *tarkas* together with drums, as would be done in Conima or indigenous Bolivian communities. In the second set, Grupo Aymara performed repetitive indigenous pieces without planned contrasts or development and reproduced the rougher-edged, denser instrumental timbres favored by indigenous communities, thereby presenting a closer facsimile of the source styles (CD tracks 1–8).

In effect, the trajectory I am referring to is a subjective one, and it goes like this. Based on values of eclecticism and openness, or a search for roots, cosmopolitans are often attracted to sounds and styles that are new or exotic. But since musical tastes are shaped by experience up to that time, the new style must also somehow resemble music people are familiar with, as a point of entry, to be attractive. As listeners become accustomed to the new sound—of, say, a *kena* albeit played with European technique—their musical taste expands (they "stretch their ears") and they are gradually prepared for new, even more distinctive, musical sounds and approaches—an indigenous *kena* player, a *siku* ensemble, a *pinkillu* ensemble. And so it goes. Coupled with the valuing of authenticity, which is a stock part of folkloric discourse, people who are invested in a particular type of music may find themselves seeking out ever more original, or "esoteric," sources for the cosmopolitan re-creation that had initially peaked their interest.

I think that many of us who teach 'world music' classes hope that our students will become engaged with these same processes of "ear stretching" and will be inspired to dig deeper into the nature, history, and performance of the musics that they are attracted to. This was certainly my trajectory with Andean music. I began by hearing the Paris-based group Urubamba on a record produced and championed by mainstream pop star Paul Simon. It led me to Cusco, where I began studying *mestizo* music with Julio Benavente—a far cry from Urubamba but more similar to music I knew than indigenous Quechua singing or Aymara *pinkillu* music. Ultimately, I landed in Conima, Peru, where indigenous friends taught me the deep joys and satisfactions of playing communal participatory music—a type that defies reproduction on recordings or concert stages because it is as much about the doing and the social relations realized through performance as it is about the medium of sound. And so I came to understand that the English noun "music" can refer to radically different types of phenomena, not just in the sense that there are multiple sound styles but in a deeper ontological sense of truly different existences. This lesson alone was worth the trip.

Glossary

Altiplano High plain; in Peru it refers to regions in the Department of Puno.

Antara Quechua term for panpipe. In central and northern Peru it usually refers to a single-row panpipe.

Arca "The one that follows." This term refers to the seven-tube row of a two-row panpipe or siku.

Ayllu An Andean term used to refer to indigenous communities or social/political units.

Aymara A major indigenous Andean language spoken in southern Peru and Bolivia.

Bombo A relatively large double-headed drum. In the Aymara context of Conima the term (also *wankara*) refers to the drums used to accompany sikus. *Bombo* also refers to a smaller double-headed Argentinean drum used in Andean "folkloric" ensembles.

Cadence Like punctuation marks in language, the term refers to a musical gesture that signals the end of a phrase, section, or piece. A "partial cadence" can be likened to a comma in a sentence, and a "full cadence" is like a period marking the end of a sentence.

Charango Andean stringed instrument modeled on the Spanish guitar (or *vihuela*), although much smaller in size. It has between four and twenty strings divided into four or five courses. Regional tunings abound.

Chicha A genre of Peruvian urban music that is a combination of *wayno* melody and form with *cumbia* rhythm performed with electric instruments and Caribbean percussion. In the 1980s and 1990s its primary audience was highland migrants in cities and especially the children of Andean migrants.

Chillador A synonym for small, high-pitched *charangos*.

Choclo A fast *siku* genre performed in Conima for Easter, like a *ligero* except that snare and bass drums replace the *bombos*.

Chokela A large end-notched fluted used in Puno, Peru, and elsewhere. Like a *kena*, only larger.

Chuta chuta Fast-cadence figures at the end of phrases in the *ligero* and *choclo* genres in Conima.

Consort A group of instruments made and tuned to be played together.

Cosmopolitan A type of cultural formation that is widely geographically diffused across different countries but sometimes only involves certain portions of the population of given countries. The modernist-capitalist and Islamic cosmopolitan formations are two primary examples of the type in the contemporary period. Like all cultural formations, the members are united by a variety of shared habits of thought and practice.

Criollo In Peru this social category connotes Euro-Peruvian or strong Spanish heritage. It is a higher-prestige category relative to mestizos and indigenous people.

Cultural cohort A subculture or smaller identity unit embedded in, and for which the conditions are set by, the larger cultural formation of which it is part.

Cumbia A song–dance genre from Colombia in duple meter. As performed by a variety of ensemble types, it became widely diffused throughout the Americas.

Department In Peru this term refers to a geographical/political unit like a state in the United States.

Discourse Following the work of social theorist Michel Foucault, the term is used here to refer to a system of premises and terms used to conceptualize and communicate about a particular realm of life, activity, or problem, as in "feminist discourse," "academic discourse," "nationalist discourse." One of Foucault's great insights was that the premises and terms of a discourse bring each other into existence and sustain each other to shape worldview. For example, the term 'nation' is imbued with its meaning (culture group with a right to its own sovereignty) by the premises of nationalism (each cultural group has a right to its own sovereignty).

Ethnic A general designation for cultural group. In the contemporary period, the term tends to be used to refer to minority or subaltern groups residing within nation-states to indicate their subnational status. Thus, when an 'ethnic' group seeks or gains control over its own territory and government (its own state), it ceases to be an 'ethnic' group and becomes a 'nation.' The meaning and logic of these identity designations are often determined by, and best understood in relation to, the discourse of nationalism.

Field of Practice Drawn from the work of social theorist Pierre Bourdieu, a social field of practice is defined by (1) the type of activity involved (e.g., "economic field," "field of agricultural production," "musical field," "participatory music field"); (2) the social roles and relationships of actors; and (3) the goals, values, and "rules of the game" determining the nature (and status) of roles and practices within the field.

Folkloric Of the folk. Both the terms 'folk' and 'folkloric' derive from nationalist and modernist-cosmopolitan discourses. These terms are typically used by cosmopolitans to refer to people and practices regarded as noncosmopolitan and not-modern. Left to their own devices, few people designated as 'folk' by cosmopolitans would self-identify as such. As used in this book, the term refers to cosmopolitan contexts and practices that reference noncosmopolitan indigenous and mestizo arts and practices.

Formulas In Aymara music, a preexisting melodic unit or motive that can be "plugged into" different pieces of a genre in a given part of the melody, such as formulas used to conclude a section (cadence formulas) or opening formulas.

Guía Guide. The term is used for the informal (in Conima) and more hierarchical (in Lima) leaders of Conimeño wind ensembles.

Hacienda A large farm or ranch, usually involved with cash crop production.

Hacendado Owner of a large ranch or farm.

Heterophony Two or more voices or instruments performing variants of a melody simultaneously such that they are not in strict unison.

Icon A *sign* (see below) that calls something else to mind through some type of resemblance. A drawing of a dragon is an iconic sign for the idea "dragon."

Imillani A dance and *siku* genre for the "coming out" of young girls.

Index A *sign* (see below) that calls something else to mind because the perceiver has experienced the sign and what it stands for together. Smoke is an index of fire. The "Wedding March" is an index for weddings and marriage.

Indigenismo Indianist movement. A generic term to refer to a variety of middle-class Peruvian social movements that were concerned with indigenous peoples and cultural practices.

Ira The one that leads. This term refers to the six-tube row of a two-row panpipe or *siku*.

Kashua A pre-Columbian generic term referring to indigenous Andean circle dances.

Kena Indigenous vertical end-notched flute of pre-Columbian origin.

Marinera A Peruvian mestizo song–dance genre in 6/8-3/4 meter and favoring the major mode. The songs are strophic and the musical form is sectional, e.g., AABBCB; the entire form is repeated twice. It is a flirtatious couples dance and is related historically and stylistically to the *cueca Chilena* and the Bolivian *cueca*.

Mestizo A social category in the Andes implying a mixture of European and indigenous heritage. Whereas it was once used as a racial category, it is now better understood as a cultural/class category implying a mixture of Iberian and indigenous cultural habits.

Nation A general designation for a cultural group and/or identity unit that has or, according to nationalist discourse, has a right to its own state (territory and government).

Pachamama Indigenous concept of the Earth as a vital, living, feminine life force.

Participatory Music This refers to music-making contexts in which there are no clear artist/audience distinctions, in which the success of performance is judged by the degree of participation (in playing, singing, dancing) achieved, and in which participants at all skill levels are welcomed to participate together in the same performance. It is music *for doing*.

Pinkillu Vertical duct flute, Aymara pronunciation.

Pinkullu Vertical duct flute, Quechua pronunciation.

Pitu Name in Conima for an indigenous cane transverse flute.

Presentational Music This is music produced by one group of people (the artists/performers) for another group (the audience). This is music *for listening*.

Puna High-altitude regions above the tree line in the Andes.

Punchay Kashua "Day" circle dance performed in Canas during public festivals.

Quechua The most widely spoken indigenous Andean language.

Siku Double-row panpipe in which the pitch series is divided between the two rows.

Sikumoreno A mestizo style of double-row panpipe performance in Puno. Often colorful "costumes of light" are worn by performers during festivals; the panpipes are accompanied by snare and bass drums and cymbals. The style resembles the *choclo* genre of Conima.

Satiri A *siku* genre and costumed dance drama that enacts the annual agricultural cycle in Conima.

Sign As defined by C. S. Peirce, something (anything) that stands for (calls to mind) something else to someone in some way.

Sirena Mermaid, siren.

Suyo "Quarter," refers to the division of the Inca Empire into four quarters.

Tarkas Wooden duct flutes originally from Bolivia, used in Conima, Peru, for Carnival.

Timbre Sound quality that distinguishes one instrument from another and, more subtly, one singer's voice from another. Pressing the bow down hard on violin strings produces a different timbre from light bowing. Metal-string *charangos* have a different timbre from nylon-string *charangos*.

T'inka A ritual involving offerings of alcohol and coca leaves to indigenous Andean divinities and social communion through the offering of coca leaves.

Tinya A small, hand-held drum used in the central Peruvian Andes and often played by women.

Tuta Kashua "Night" circle dance performed in private parties among young people in Canas.

Vals Criollo "Criollo waltz," originally a working-class genre popular in the early 20th century in Lima, and often performed with one or two guitars as a vocal solo or duet. Over the course of the twentieth century it became a musical emblem for *criollos* in Lima more generally.

Vidala A slow, lyrical Argentinean song genre in 6/8 meter. It is related stylistically to the Peruvian *yaraví*.

Wayno (Huayno) The most important genre of highland mestizo music, usually in short sectional forms such as AABB or AABBCC, with a major–minor bimodal quality, in simple duple meter and a characteristic rhythm that subtly moves between an eighth-two-sixteenth-note rhythm and an eighth-note triplet. The term refers to regionally specific dances and to a strophic song. In indigenous communities the term is sometimes used in the very broad sense of denoting "music" or "song."

Wayno Lento A slow dance genre performed on *sikus* in Conima.

Wayno Ligero A fast dance genre performed on *sikus* in Conima.

Yaraví A slow, lyrical, strophic song genre in 6/8-3/4 meter. The texts often refer to loss, romantic love, and nostalgia for home.

References

Albó, Javier. 1974. La paradoja Aymara: solidaridad y faccionalismo. *Estudios Andinos* 4 (2): 67–110.

Altamirano, Teófilo. 1984. *Presencia Andina en Lima Metropolitana: Un Studio Sobre Migrantes y Clubes de Provincianos.* Lima: Pontificia Universidad Católica del Perú.

Arguedas, José María. 1977. *Formación de una Cultura Nacional Indoamericana.* Mexico City: Siglo Veintiuno Editores S.A.

Bigenho, Michelle. 2002. *Sounding Indigenous: Authenticity in Bolivian Music Performance.* New York: Palgrave.

Cánepa-Koch, Gisela. 1995. *Traditional Music of Peru*, vol. 1: *Festivals of Cusco*, Smithsonian/Folkways CD, booklet.

d'Harcourt, Raoul, and Marguerite d'Harcourt. 1925. *La Musique des Incas et Ses Survivances.* Paris: Libraire Orientaliste Paul Geuthner.

Feld, Steven. 1988. "Aesthetics as Iconicity of Style, or 'Lift-Up-Over Sounding': Getting into the Kaluli Groove." *Yearbook for Traditional Music* 20:74—113.

Feldman, Heidi. 2006. *Black Rhythms of Peru: Reviving African Musical Heritage in the Black Pacific.* Middletown, CT: Wesleyan University Press.

Gow, David D. 1974. 'Taytacha Qoyllur Rit'I. *Allpanchis Phuturinqa* 7:49–100.

Hall, Edward. 1977. *Beyond Culture.* Garden City, NY: Anchor Books.

Laos, Cipriano A. 1929. *Lima: La Ciudad de los Virreyes.* Lima: Touring Club Peruano and Editorial Peru.

Llórens, José Antonio. 1983. *Música Popular en Lima: Criollos y Andinos.* Lima: Instituto de Estudios Peruanos.

———. 1985. Los "programas folklóricos" en la radiodifusion limeña. In *Materiales para la Comunicación Popular.* Lima: Centro de Estudios sobre Cultura Transnacional.

McNeill, William H. 1995. *Keeping Together in Time: Dance and Drill in Human History.* Cambridge, MA: Harvard University Press.

Meisch, Lynn A. 2002. *Andean Entrepreneurs: Otavalo Merchants and Musicians in the Global Arena.* Austin: University of Texas Press.

Mendoza Walker, Zoila S. 2000. *Shaping Society Through Dance: Mestizo Ritual Performance in the Peruvian Andes*. Chicago: University of Chicago Press.

Merriam, Alan. 1964. *The Anthropology of Music*. Evanston, IL: Northwestern University Press.

Mishkin, Bernard. 1946. The contemporary Quechua. In *The Handbook of South American Indians*, vol. 2. *The Andean Civilizations*, ed. Julian Steward. Washington, D.C.: Government Printing Office.

Moore, Robin. 1997. *Nationalizing Blackness: Afrocubanismo and Artistic Revolution in Havana, 1920–1940*. Pittsburgh: University of Pittsburgh Press.

Nettl, Bruno. 1964. *Theory and Method in Ethnomusicology*. Urbana: University of Illinois Press.

Rios, Fernando. 2005. Music in urban La Paz, Bolivian nationalism, and the early history of cosmopolitan Andean music: 1936–1970. PhD diss., University of Illinois at Urbana-Champaign.

———. n.d. *La Flute Indienne:* The early history of Andean folkloric music in France and its impact on *Nueva Canción*. Unpublished ms.

Romero, Raul. 2001. *Debating the Past: Music, Memory, and Identity in the Andes*. New York: Oxford University Press.

———. 2002 Popular music and the global city: huayno, chicha, and techno-cumbia in Lima. In *From Tejano to Tango: Latin American Popular Music*, ed. W. A. Clark, 217–239. New York: Routledge.

Schaedel, Richard P. 1974. From homogenization to heterogenization in Lima, Peru. *Urban Anthropology* 8 (3/4): 399–420.

Sheehy, Daniel. 2006. *Mariachi Music in America: Experiencing Music, Expressing Culture*. New York: Oxford University Press.

Solomon, Thomas J. 1997. Mountains of song: musical constructions of ecology, place, and identity, in the Bolivian Andes. PhD diss., University of Texas at Austin.

Stobart, Henry. 2002. Interlocking realms: knowing music and musical knowing in the Bolivian Andes. In *Knowledge and Learning in the Andes*, ed. Henry Stobart and Rosaleen Howard, 79–108. Liverpool: Liverpool University Press.

———. 1998. Bolivia. In *The Garland Encyclopedia of World Music*, vol. 2: *South America, Mexico, Central America, and the Caribbean,* ed. by Dale A. Olsen and Daniel E. Sheehy, 282–299. New York: Garland Publishing Inc.

Turino, Thomas. 1993. *Moving Away from Silence: Music of the Peruvian Altiplano and the Experience of Urban Migration*. Chicago: University of Chicago Press.

———. 2008. *Musical Meaning and Social Participation*. Chicago: University of Chicago Press.

Vianna, Hermano. 1999. *The Mystery of Samba: Popular Music and National Identity in Brazil*, Chapel Hill: University of North Carolina Press.

Villasante Ortiz, Segundo. 1980 Paucartambo: Provincia Folklorica Mamacha Carmen, Tomo II. Cusco: Editorial Leon.

Vivanco, J. Alejandro. 1973. El migrante de provincias como intérprete del folklore Andino en Lima. B.A. thesis, Universidad Nacional Mayor de San Marcos, Lima.

Wade, Bonnie C. 2004. *Thinking Musically: Experiencing Music, Expressing Culture*. New York: Oxford University Press.

Weber, Max. 1958. *The Protestant Ethic and the Spirit of Capitalism*. New York: Charles Scribner's Sons.

Resources

Reading: Journals and Reference Works

Latin American Music Review.

Ethnomusicology.

Olsen, Dale, and Daniel Sheehy, eds. 1998. *The Garland Encyclopedia of World Music*, vol. 2: *South America, Mexico, Central America, and the Caribbean.* New York: Garland Publishing. See country articles.

Sadie, Stanley, ed. 2000. *The New Grove Dictionary of Music and Musicians.* London: Macmillan Publishers. See country articles.

Reading: Books and Articles

Béhague, Gerard. 1979. *Music in Latin America: An Introduction.* Englewood Cliffs, NJ: Prentice Hall.

Romero, Raul. 1998. Peru. In *The Garland Encyclopedia of World Music*, vol. 2: *South America, Mexico, Central America, and the Caribbean*, ed. Dale Olsen and Daniel Sheehy. New York: Garland Publishing.

Schechter, John. 1991. *The Indispensable Harp: Historical Development, Modern Roles, Configurations, and Performance Practices in Ecuador and Latin America.* Kent, OH: Kent State University Press.

———. 1998. Ecuador. In *The Garland Encyclopedia of World Music*, vol. 2: *South America, Mexico, Central America, and the Caribbean*, ed. Dale Olsen and Daniel Sheehy. New York: Garland Publishing.

Stevenson, Robert. 1968. *Music in Aztec and Inca Territory.* Berkeley: University of California Press.

Stobart, Henry. 1998. Bolivia. In *The Garland Encyclopedia of World Music*, vol. 2: *South America, Mexico, Central America, and the Caribbean*, ed. Dale A. Olsen and Daniel E. Sheehy, 282–299. New York: Garland Publishing.

———. 2006. *Music and the Poetics of Production in the Bolivian Andes.* London: Ashgate Publishing.

Turino, Thomas. 2003. Nationalism and Latin American music: selected cases and theoretical considerations. *Latin American Music Review* 24 (2): 169–209.

Listening

From the Mountains to the Sea: Music of Peru — The 1960s, Arhoolie 400. 1996.
Huayno Music of Peru, vol. 1, Arhoolie CD 320. 1998.
Indian Music of the Upper Amazon, Folkways FW4458.
Instruments and Music of Indians of Bolivia, Folkways FW0412.
Inti-illimani 4: Alborada Vendra, Monitor MFS 794.
Quilapayún, Monitor MON00773. 1954.
Mountain Music of Peru, vol. 1, Smithsonian/Folkways SFW40020.
Mountain Music of Peru, vol. 2, Smithsonian/Folkways SFW40406.
Music of Peru, Folkways FW04415. 1950.
Musik im Andenhochland, Bolivien, Museum Collection Berlin (West) MC14.
The Inca Harp: Laments and Dances of the Tawantinsuyu, the Inca Empire, Lyrichord LLST 7359. 1980.
Traditional Music of Peru, Folkways FW04456. 1958.
Traditional Music of Peru, vol. 1: *Festivals of Cusco,* Smithsonian/Folkways SFW40466. 1995.
Traditional Music of Peru, vol. 2: *The Mantaro Valley,* Smithsonian/Folkways SFW40467. 1985.
Traditional Music of Peru, vol.3: *Cajamarca and the Colca Valley,* Smithsonian/Folkways SFW40468. 1997.
Traditional Music of Peru, vol. 4: *Lambayeque,* Smithsonian/Folkways SFW40469. 1996.
Traditional Music of Peru, vol. 5: *Celebrating Divinity in the High Andes,* Smithsonian/Folkways SFW40448. 1999.
Traditional Music of Peru, vol. 6: *The Ayacucho Region,* Smithsonian/Folkways SFW40449. 2001.
Traditional Music of Peru, vol. 7: *The Lima Highlands,* Smithsonian/Folkways SFW40450. 2001.
Traditional Music of Peru, vol. 8: *Piura,* Smithsonian/Folkways SFW40451. p 2002.
Uña Ramos: La Flute des Andes, Harmonia Mundi (France) LDX 74 585. 1975.
Urubamba, Colombia Records KG 32896. 1974.
Your Struggle Is Your Glory: Songs of Struggle, Huayno & Other Peruvian Music, Arhoolie 3025. 1988.

Video

Cohen, John. *Mountain Music of Peru.* Berkeley: University of California Extension Center for Media and Independent Learning. Video.
———. *Dancing with the Incas.* Berkeley: University of California Extension Center for Media and Independent Learning. Video.
———. *Carnival in Q'eros.* Berkeley: University of California Extension Center for Media and Independent Learning. Video.

Index

Abalos Brothers, 130–131
accordion, 77–78, 104
Afro-Peruvian music, 123
agriculture and music, 36, 52, 83
Albó, Javier, 7
Alencastre, Andrés, 38, 58, 60
Allende, President Salvador, 135
Alomía Robles, Daniel, 132
Ancash (Department of): migrants in Lima, 104, 108; musical style, 104–106, 123
Antisuyo, 87
Aquachilenos, 72, 75, 80
arca, 8
Arequipa, 62
Argentina, 127, 131
Ayacucho (Department of): migrants in Lima, 104, 108; musical style, 104, 106
Aymara language, 4
Aymara music, 1–37; compared with Quechua music, 39–42; general style features, 17–20, 24–26
Aymara musical instruments. *See kena; pinkillu; pitu; siku; tarka*
Aymara social relations, 6–8
Aymara spiritual beliefs, 27, 28, 33

bailecitos, 131
bandurria, 42
battles (dramatic/ritual), 85–85
Beatles, 136
Benavente Díaz, Julio, 54–58, 60, 61–62, 67–68, 102, 126–127, 138
Bohorquez, Raul, 68
Bolivia, 3, 15, 22, 38, 52–54, 75, 89, 121, 127, 131; La Paz, 135

bombo, xii, 9, 125, 131, 133, 137
brass bands, 16, 77, 79, 80
Brazil, 121, 122, 136
Buenos Aires, 130–131

cajas, 13, 29
Calderón, Aldamir, 9
Calderón, Filiberto, 9, 20
Canas (Province of), 38–42; musical comparison with Conima, 39–42, 63
Canchis (Province of), 42
capitalism, 98
Caribbean percussion, 118, 120, 122
Castle, Vernon and Irene, 130
Cavour, Ernesto, 135
Centro Qosqo de Arte Nativo, 62, 102
Centro Social Conima, 111–117
charango, xii; description of, 42–44; in folkloric Andean music, 124–127, 131–135, 137; indigenous performance, 21, 43–54, 68–69; *mestizo* performance, 57–64, 68–69, 104; origins of, 38
Chaón, Augusto, 61
Chicago blues, 97
chicha music, 118–121, 122, 123, 127
Chile, 127
chillador, 48
choclo, 11,36
chokela. See kena
Chukchus, 75
Chunchos, 71–72, 73, 75, 80, 83, 85–86; description of, 87–88
chuta chuta, 10, 11
clarinet, 104
classical music, xi, 123
coliseos, 106–107, 109

151

Collasuyo, 89
Columbia, 118
competition (musical), 31–32
composition (musical), 17, 29, 34
Conima (District of), 1–3, 5, 40, 121;
    migrants in Lima, 111–118;
    musical comparison with Canas,
    39–42, 63; musicians in Lima,
    103, 109
contra dance, 87
cosmopolitism, 39, 69–70, 97, 105; as a
    cultural formation, 127–138
country music (U.S.), 97, 103, 105, 108
criollo, xii, 5, 38, 56, 57, 97, 99, 111.
    See also social groups/identities;
    vals criollo
Cuban son, 130, 136
cueca, 125, 133
Cugat, Xavier, 132
cultural cohort, 129–130
cumbia, xi–xii, 118, 122
Cusco (City of), xi, 54–56, 62, 102,
    124, 127
Cusco (Department of), 39–40, 74,
    105; migrants in Lima, 106, 108

dance drama, 12, 13, 33–37; defined, 74
dancing, 15, 21, 22, 26, 30–31;
    presentational 'folk,' 63
Destellos, Los, 118
Doctores, 72, 75; description of, 94–95
duct flutes, 38. See also pinkillu;
    pinkullu; tarka

Ecuador, 3, 38, 131, 136
egalitarian relations, 7, 25
"El Condor Pasa" (song), 126, 132–134
electric guitar, xi, 118, 122, 136.
    See also guitar
elite Peruvian composers, 99–100,
    102, 130
emotion and music, 10, 14

Favre, Gilbert, 134–135
Festival of Año Nuevo, 14, 26–32
Festival of Candelaria, 14, 26, 36
Festival of Carnival, 1, 13, 14, 15, 26,
    31, 36

Festival of Christmas, 12
Festival of Easter, 36
Festival of San Isidro, 26, 33–37
Festival of San Miguel, 9
Festival Santa Cruz, 12
Festival of Todos los Santos, 13, 26
Festival of Virgin of Carmen, 71–96;
    social function of, 81
folk revivals, 129, 136–137
folkloric (concept of), 62, 94
'folkloric Andean style,' xii, 20, 70,
    122, 124–138; instrumentation,
    131, 133, 135, 137
folkloric contests, 100–101, 114
fuga, 66, 128
Fujimori, President Alberto, 121
funk, 122
futbol (soccer), 111,112

gatos, 134
gender and music, 22, 40–42, 76, 121
globalization, 39
Godoy, Julio, 135
Gomez, Negrón Pancho, 58–59
Grupo Aymara, 137
Guaranís, Los, 131
Guardia, Jaime, 58
guía, 23, 31
guitar, xii, 38, 59, 68, 104, 125, 133,
    137. See also electric guitar
guitarrón, 42

hacienda, 55–56, 93–94
Harcourt, Marguerite and
    Raoul d', 130
harp, 38, 77, 104
hippie tourists, 75, 127
Huancané (Province of), 5
huayno. See wayno

imillani, 11,33
Incas, xi; festivals, 83, 86; idealized
    image of, 99–103, 105, 126, 128,
    130; social organization, 87
Incas, Los (folkloric ensemble),
    131–133
Indigenismo, 38, 57–58, 61–63,
    100–102, 127, 130, 132

indigenous instruments:
    pre-Columbian, 38; seasonal
    associations, 9, 12, 13
Inti-Illimani, 135
ira, 8

Jairas, Los, 135
jazz, xi, 123, 130, 131, 136
Joffré, Edgar Yayo, 135
joropo, 134
Joven Sensacíon, 122
Junin (Department of): migrants in
    Lima, 104, 108; musical style,
    104, 106

Kjarkas, Los, 135–136
kena, xii, 14; context of use, 100, 104;
    description of 15, 17; in folkloric
    Andean music, 124–127, 131–135,
    137; *mestizo* performance, 57,
    77–78; performance context, 21,
    54–55, 56
keyboards, 118, 122, 136
Kingston Trio, 137

"La Bamba" (song), 134
learning music, 21, 24, 116
Leguía, President Augusto, 98, 100–101
L'Ensemble Achalay, 131
lento. See wayno lento
ligero. See wayno ligero
Lima, 62; demographics, 99; music
    100–123

Majeños, 72, 74, 75, 80; description
    of, 92
mandolin, 38, 77
maps, 6
Maqtas, 85
mariachi, 66, 136
marinera, 66, 76, 82, 133
merengue, 136
Merriam, Alan, 124
mestizo, xii, 5, 38, 57, 72; spiritual
    beliefs, 56, 81, 83
Mexican *son*, 66
migration (rural to urban), 97–98;
    highland migrants in Lima, 103–118

Milchberg, Jorge, 126, 133
modernity (discourse of), 98, 115, 128

nationalism, 57–58, 61–63, 69, 94, 98,
    99–103, 120–121, 136; folkloric
    events, 94, 99, 100–101, 103
Nettl, Bruno, 124
nueva canción, 135

opera, 99
Orquesta: of Ancash, 104; of Cusco, 77,
    79, 80, 104, 126; of Junin, 104

Pachamama, 26, 81–82
Paniagua, 58
panpipes. *See siku*
papa tarpuy, 52
Paris, 130–131, 134–135
Parra, Angel, 134–135
Parra, Isabel, 134–135
Parra, Violeta, 134–135
participatory performance, xiii–xiv,
    4, 20–26, 39, 61–64, 68, 82, 106,
    128–129, 134
pasacalle, 76
Pastorita Huaracina, 105, 126–127
peña ('folk' club), 130–131, 134,
    135, 136
Peter, Paul and Mary, 137
pinkillu, 40; description, 13–14;
    performance context, 13, 14, 29–30,
    36, 113; performance style, 13
pinkullu, 13; description, 40–41;
    performance context, 42;
    performance style, 40–42
pitu: ensembles, 12; instrument, 12;
    musical style, 13; performance
    context, 12
pre-Columbian music, 13, 38
presentational performance, xiii–xiv,
    21–22, 25, 39, 61–64, 68, 69, 82,
    106, 128–129, 134
processions (Catholic), 83–85
Puno (Department of), 5, 64, 73, 89;
    migrants in Lima, 108, 110–118

Qhapaq Negros, 72, 74, 75, 80;
    description of, 92

Qollas, 71–72, 75, 80, 85–86; description of, 89
Quechua (language), 4, 56, 103
Quechua and Aymara music compared, 39–42
Quechua musical instruments. *See charango; pinkullu; bandurria*
Quechua social relations, 40
quena. See kena
Quilapayún, 135

radio, 103, 108–109
Ramos, Uña, 124–126
rap, 122
recordings (highland music in Lima), 107–108
regional associations, 110–118; festivals, 114
Rios, Fernando, 130–135
rock music, xi, 122–123; Andean fusion, 136
Ruphay, Los, 137

samba-reggae, 122
sanjuanito, 136
Saqras, 72, 74, 75, 80, 84–86; description of, 91–92
satiri, 33–37
Savia Andina, 135
saxophone, 104
saya, 136
sesquialtera (hemiola), 66
Shapis, Los, 119–120, 127
Sheehy, Daniel, 66
siku: description of, 8; in folkloric Andean music, 135, 137; performance contexts, 113, 114, 127; performance technique, 25; siku ensembles, 9, 103. *See also choclo; imillani; satiri; wayno ligero; wayno lento*
signs (musical), 25, 26, 52, 56, 68, 103–104, 105, 113, 120, 128
Simon and Garfunkel, 126, 133
Simon, Paul, 126, 133, 137, 138
sirena (mermaid), 47
social groups/identity, xii, 4–6, 9, 20, 38–39, 40, 75; among children

of migrants, 119–120; hierarchal relations, 56–57, 63, 99, 102, 105, 111, regional identities, 103–110, 120–121
specialization (musical), 23, 24
street musicians, 126, 136
suyos, 87

tango, 131, 136
tarka, 1, 14; description of, 14; in folkloric Andean music, 137; performance contexts, 15, 113, 123; performance style, 14–15
technocumbia, 121–123
t'inka ritual, 27, 36
tinya, 22
tourism, 137
trumpet, 122
tuta kashua, 45, 47–51

Urubamba (folkloric ensemble), 124–129

vals criollo, 69, 123
Velasco, President Juan, 98, 103, 112
vidala, 125, 133
vihuela, 42
violin, 38, 77–78, 104
Virgin of Carmen, 71, 81–82, 83–85, 90–91
vocal music, 40–42

wankara. See bombo
wayno (huayno): in Chicha, 118, 120; commercialization of in Lima, 103–110, 123; in folkloric Andean music, 127, 128, 131, 133; *mestizo* genre, 64, 66, 76, 82, 100, 101, 103, 125, 131
wayno lento, 10–11, 33
wayno ligero, 10–11, 33
Weber, Max, 128

yaraví, 66, 100, 125, 131, 133
Yawar, 136

zamba, 134
zarzuela, 132